PREFACE

F or those of you who read my first book, There's a Meth Head in Your Dryer, you will find that you have already read the bulk of this preface, but with a couple of changes. These first few paragraphs, however, were added for everyone, whether you have read the first volume or not. The first book was really just a litmus test, designed to see just how much I could get away with and to get a feel of how these stories would be received. I intentionally left out the rougher narratives and I also chose not to tell you about many of the times that I lost my temper with these fugitives. But due to the positive feedback of the first book, I have obviously underestimated my readers' thirst for violence and need to live vicariously through the suffering of others.

Because of those facts, I have held very little back in this second volume. I have even decided to share a few new elements of this job with you, such as some notes, signs, and threats that I have encountered. And don't worry, I have thrown in some new phone calls, as well. So, if you were at all shocked or surprised about my previous tales, strap in tight for this second installment. If book one made you question whether or not you are a bad person for laughing at these stories, book two should easily provide you with the final answer to that query. But don't lie to yourself, because you enjoy reading about it just much as I love writing it.

Before we get into the meat and potatoes of all of this, I think it's important to get the only boring part of this book out of the way and let you know what brought me here. There wasn't much going on in West Virginia when I graduated in 1988. My dad and his brother were well respected state troopers, so my childhood was filled with criminals and great stories about all sorts of crimes. When I was young, they used to sit around telling stories and laughing about what seemed to me, at the time, the most terrible stories. It took growing up, eight years in the Army and several deployments for me to understand why they laughed so hard at those stories. I have learned that if you can't find humor in a bad situation, you could easily end up becoming a miserable person. If you disagree with me there, you are reading the wrong book.

Among other places, the Army sent me to Germany, Korea, and Iraq, where I served in Operation Desert Storm with the 101st Airborne. When I got out of the military, my dad had retired and was working as a private investigator. I eventually went to work for him, but not until after I had tried a few regular jobs and learned that "normal life" just wasn't for me.

I sold furniture in Ohio for a short time, where I had to wear a shirt and tie. That ended abruptly when I got into a fight with a female coworker's husband after he came into the store and hit her. I couldn't believe how the other male employees stood by and did nothing, but I was okay with the outcome. I made airplane parts at a factory in Georgia for a short time, but it was wildly mismanaged, and I couldn't stand watching simple problems being left unsolved. I also spent a few months at a tool rental company there, and I even worked in Atlanta for a video gambling company. My real passion had always been art, but I could never imagine doing it for a living. The Army can debrief you all they want, but the things I had learned and experienced clearly weren't going anywhere.

I ended up landing back in WV and getting my private investigator's license. My dad had his foot in the door with the Workman's Compensation Fraud Unit, so I immediately began investigating for them. I spent my time following claimants who were suspected of lying about physical injuries. I was very successful, and at one point I was turning in more video than all the other investigators combined. This led to repeatedly testifying in court, working with attorneys, and I even worked several federal cases for a major railroad company.

It wasn't long before I got a solid job offer closer to home that meant much better hours, and less traveling. That's where this all really started. It was a job investigating crimes for a prominent local defense attorney, and I accepted. For several years, I worked closely with criminals charged with every crime imaginable. Working on cases involving violent crimes like rape, drive-by shootings, and child abuse were part of my day-to-day activities.

One evening I got a call from a bail bond company wanting to hire me to locate a fugitive for them. They had searched for months with no luck, and someone had recommended that they call me. To make a long story short, they hired me, I found the guy in a few hours, and they offered me a full-time job. I took it, and here we are today. All the experience I had with criminals had given me a unique understanding of human nature and made me a perfect fit for the bail bond industry.

The wanted posters I have placed on social media over the years have made quite the stir in my area. They have incited every sort of argument you can imagine and got my accounts banned countless times, but they have also been very successful. I am going to share many of those posters with you in this book. I was even sued once, and over 125 legal exhibits were my social media posts. There were always more supporters than haters and I expect the same wide spectrum of reactions to this book. Please understand that there is no room for weakness in the criminal world and trying to cater to these new "woke" agendas can get you killed. I have been shot, stabbed, and had plastic surgery on my face since I got into this business. I have seen folks quit this job in less than a week. I even had a guy make me let him out of the car on the way to his first arrest. Believe me when I tell you that this life is nothing like how they make it look on terrible television shows. Whatever you think, I hope that you will find the humor in these true experiences that I'm about to share with you.

Any comments about these stories, positive or negative, are both welcome and appreciated. Whether you have a funny observation, or just want to cuss me out, you can email me at garyvaughansbook@gmail.com.

TABLE OF CONTENTS

1. HOW BAIL BONDS WORK
2. WHOSE COKE IS THIS?
3. SKINNY & FATTY
4. SKINNY & FATTY 2
5. CRACK BABY
6. WHORE DEMOGRAPHICS 101
7. TWO PADLOCKS & A HOUSE FIRE
8. HARRY & BO
9. FUCK YOUR DOOR
10. MY KIDNAPPER GOT KIDNAPPED
11. JAMES & JAMIE
12. VACUUM CLEANER
13. I DIDN'T KILL HIM, YOU DID!
14. DIRTBAG IRONY
15. CRIMINAL CASE STORIES
16. NOBODY HAS A KNIFE LIKE THAT
17. IT STILL HURTS WHEN I PEE
18. LONG-DISTANCE DOUBLE-CROSS
19. SHORT STORIES
20. BITCH ON A STICK
21. YOU TOTALED MY JEEP
22. FISH FUCKERS REVISITED

HOW BAIL BONDS WORK

Very quickly, it's important that you understand exactly what a bail bond is. Bail works a little different in varying states but the basics rarely change. For the purposes of this book, you really only need to know the following: For easy math, if you are arrested with a $10,000 bond, you have four options.

1. Sit your ass in jail and wait for a court date. No one wants to do this.

2. A loved one or friend can put their home up as collateral, if it's paid for. You cannot use your own in most states, so it must be a third party. Most folks cannot make this happen.

3. You, or someone else, can pay the court the full $10,000, which will be returned in full when your case is complete. Most cannot do this either.

4. You can use a bail bond company, who will charge you 10% in most cases. You pay that company $1,000 and they put up the $10,000 for you. When your case is over, your business is complete, and you have remained out of jail the entire time. If you miss a court date or flee, they

are going to protect their $10,000 by finding you, arresting you, and placing you into jail.

Until recently, most states have had very few regulations governing bail bond companies and fugitive recovery. Most regulations have been very relaxed, with far less rules to follow than the police. Search warrants are not even required in most jurisdictions. Some states are so broad-minded that the laws say something to the effect of "...can return the surety to jail for any reason." The defendant is the surety and "any reason" means just that.

☻ ☻ ☻

ME: The last time I bonded you out of jail, you skipped court and ran to Texas.

HIM: Yeah, but that was completely on accident.

ME: What? Did you trip over something, fall, and land in Texas?

HIM: I swear, man, it was totally an accident.

ME: Did you fall asleep in a cattle car?

WHO'S COKE IS THIS?

An officer from the Violent Crime Task Force once called me up looking for one of my clients. The officer was also a long-time friend of mine and we had worked together many times. The defendant had violated his bond conditions with the court and a new warrant had been issued for him. I knew right away where he lived because of all the publicity this odd case had received when it happened. You see, the defendant had been involved in a legal battle of some sort with his landlord and the two weren't supposed to have had any contact with each other. This was a recipe for disaster because the defendant was still able to live in the landlord's building until the case was resolved. I'm not sure what straw broke the camel's back, but eventually my client had shot at the landlord several times on the stairway.

He was now out on bond, still living in the same building, and was again under a no contact order with the landlord. Well, the landlord alleged that the defendant had violated that order again by waiving a gun around the building, and now here we were with new warrants. My buddy wanted me to go with him to pick this guy up. What could go wrong?

It was a small building on the side of a hill and I knew exactly which apartment was his. It was a regular shithole that I had been in dozens of times before this guy had ever even moved in there. There was no back door to the apartment and the windows were way too high to jump from, so we knew that the two of us should have been able to handle it with no problem at all. That is, except for one thing. This guy was insane. I knew him well, and it was my professional opinion that he should have been locked in a rubber room somewhere getting his meals passed through a slot in the door. I tried to make my buddy understand this on the way there, but I don't think it sank in.

We both decided that even though we had an actual warrant in hand, we would attempt to knock on the door and keep this friendly. I had a bit of a relationship with him, so I did the knocking. No guns out, just badges. He immediately came to the door, looked out the little white curtain in the diamond shaped window. "It's me, your bail bondsman," I told him. "I just need to talk to you for a minute." I thought that might get us inside, but I was wrong.

Dude's face disappeared and we heard him running back through the apartment. Well, shit.

Was he just going to go hide? Was he going to get a gun and start shooting through the door? We didn't know for sure, but we had to act fast, so I immediately kicked the door in. When I say that I kicked it in, that's exactly what I mean. The door came completely off its hinges and flew into the living room. I don't want you to think that was due to my superhuman strength or anything, because it wasn't like that at all. It simply must have been the cheapest door known to man. IKEA would have built a stronger door. Also, the apartment building itself couldn't have been built much better, because a window about four feet away from the door frame exploded at the same time the door went down. Whatever the case, we were inside within five seconds of seeing him through that little window. It was guns up and pointed now, yelling for everyone to freeze. Then things took a strange turn.

The defendant's girlfriend was standing in the center of the living room, hands up, and scared to death. The defendant was standing in the kitchen, hands up and acting squirrelly. Let me explain what I mean by that. Yeah, his hands were up, but he was about to do something stupid. His crazy eyes kept moving to his left, my right, looking into a part of the kitchen that we couldn't see. His entire body was tensed and ready to pounce. It was as if someone else was in that blind spot, or he was about to go for a gun that we couldn't see. My buddy was screaming at him to go to his knees, but he stood his ground and those loony eyes just kept on twitching. "Don't fucking do it!" I told him a few times as I inched closer.

 Just as I got close enough to tackle him, I told my buddy to cover me. I holstered my pistol and made my move. Dipshit made his move at the same time. He dove to my right, around the corner and into a spot that we couldn't see and hadn't been able to clear yet. I was committed now, so I dove in right after him. As I tackled him, he was trying to reach behind the refrigerator. His entire arm was flailing around the back of it, trying to get at something. I just knew that there was a gun back there and I couldn't let him get to it. I drug him backwards and threw the hardest punch that I could from the awkward position I was in. I landed it right on his kidney and I knew it was a good one, because I heard him gasp in pain. It hurt him long enough for me to drag him back into the center of the room. I flipped him over, handcuffed him, and sat on his back. "Get that gun from behind the fridge," I said to my buddy.

I was preaching to Dipshit about how close he just came to being shot and killed when my buddy said, "What the fuck?" I turned to see that he had pulled a full two liter of Coca-Cola from behind the fridge. Dipshit was crying now, and saying, "I'm so sorry," over and over. He might have been sorry, but we were confused. With our adrenaline still high, my buddy asked him "Did I just almost shoot you over a goddamn Coke?" Dipshit was still crying about how sorry he was and then started begging us to let him have a drink of that Coke. I am notorious for bargaining for an easier ride to jail, but this was insane. I suddenly found myself negotiating his good behavior for a drink of hot Coke. That's when the girlfriend chimed in.

"I paid for that fucking Coke and he can't have it," she yelled out. He told me that he paid for it and it was his. He was telling me this as if I were the official Coke moderator or something. "I swear that it's mine," he kept saying. Then, they both went to screaming at each other about who paid for what until I had to break it up. I had rarely seen anything quite as strange as this. Dipshit was getting arrested, a door was laying in the living room floor, there was glass all over the couch, and these two were fighting over a shitty, warm soft drink. "I will decide what the fuck happens here," I told everyone. And that's just what I did.

I concluded that we would take the entire two liter with us if he promised not to cause any more problems. I told her that we were also going to take her with us unless she sat down and shut the fuck up about the Coke. This worked out pretty well, and we got him to the car without incident. On the way to the jail, he thanked us several times for not killing him and letting him keep the Coke. He said, "That bitch would have drunk the whole damn thing while I was in jail. Fuck her, even if she did pay for it."

← →

HIM: You don't remember me, but I remember you.

ME: I'm sorry, I don't, but I hope it's a good memory.

HIM: You don't forget a guy who jumps onto your truck hood with a gun and threatens to blow your fucking head off.

ME: Oh yeah, that was a good one!

SKINNY & FATTY

Everyone at the small company I was working for was on vacation. I was the only one in town when this call came in. The caller told me where two fugitives were right this minute and gave me exact directions to where I could find them. We had been looking for these two for several months with no leads and I had honestly almost given up on them. That's why I took this call very seriously and went into immediate action.

I called everyone I knew who might be able to go with me, but no one was available. I quickly ran out of options and out of time, so I went alone. I know that making arrests alone is a terrible idea, but that was just how it had to be. I called the boss, told him about my decision, and gathered my equipment. I had decided not to take any stupid chances, and even if I was able to arrest just one of them it would be worth it. I wore my kevlar vest, grabbed my pepper spray, two pair of handcuffs, and carried my .357 Glock. Sure, the sawed off 12 gauge is scarier to look at, but it required two hands to operate. I was gonna need all the hands I could get for this one. The two were brothers and we all knew each other from doing business before. One was a skinny guy, and the other was quite overweight. Both of them were idiots. We were all actually on a first name basis, so I figured that was an advantage for me. But you can never really know how shitheads are going to react. Especially stupid ones.

The mobile home I was going to was out in the open and exposed. There was no way to sneak up on it, so the only option was to roll in hot, jump out, bust in, and see what's what. It was early on a Sunday morning and everyone knows that shitheads generally sleep in, so I figured that helped my odds. I hit the driveway as hard as the old SUV I was driving could hit it. I slid to a stop and was standing inside the living room before anyone knew I was even there. I hadn't even taken a second to shut off my engine or close my door.

So here I was, standing in the living room, looking at them both. One was standing about four feet in front of me, fully dressed, staring at me. His brother was in the kitchen with a bar separating us, holding an iron skillet, and not wearing a shirt. It was not an optimum scenario. "Drop that frying pan and put your hands where I can see them, both of you," I told them at gunpoint. There was a very weird moment to follow. It reminded me of a three-way gunfight in an old Italian western movie. I had a gun, Fatty had a frying pan, and Skinny was unarmed. We were all three exchanging glances and I could see that Skinny was thinking about making a break for it. Yeah, I have a gun, but you can't shoot a fella just for running. And you better believe that they know that. This was also very likely not the first time these two had a gun pointed at them.

"Don't fucking do it," I told him. "I swear to God that I will kill you both where you stand and plant steak knives in your hands." I ordered them to their knees but neither one complied. They were going to make this hard. I was still yelling to get on the floor when it all kicked off. Skinny took off down the hall and out the back door. Looking back on it all, I don't know why I chased him. The safe bet would have been to let him go and kick Fatty's ass if I had to. But I did chase him, and no normal thinking human could have guessed how it would all work out in the end.

The chase was on and I was gaining on him. He went across a few neighboring yards, jumped into a creek, and fell. I was even closer now and I almost caught him right there in the creek. He was crawling up the opposite bank when I jumped in, and I only missed him by less than ten feet. I didn't fall, but I dropped my gun in the water. Without even thinking, I left it behind and kept on trucking. We crossed some railroad tracks and hit some sort of parking lot. That's where I caught up to him and tackled him on the pavement. The chase was over and the fight was on.

He got a few punches in before he ended up on his back with me sitting on him and landing a few of my own. He was pretty much spent by then, but he was still trying to keep me from getting cuffs on him. I had him rolled onto his stomach but he refused to give me his hands. I was slapping the shit out of the side of his head, gave him a few kidney punches, and was calling him every name in the book. I remember it was "motherfucker this," and "motherfucker that," until I got him cuffed. That's when I realized there was a crowd gathering.

I stood him up, showed everyone my badge, and started walking him back towards home. You know, to where I had left my truck running with the door open. Someone called out, "Was all that violence necessary?" I turned around to tell them to shut the fuck up when I saw it was a preacher. I hadn't realized that we were in a church parking lot and the fight had brought the entire congregation outside. I apologized for my language, promised to repent later, and left them there saying that they were going to pray for me. I didn'thave time for this shit. I had a gun to find in the creek and likely a stolen SUV to deal with.

Finding the gun wasn't as bad as I thought. I had to slap the shit out of Skinny a few times during the process, but I found it. We had very deep conversation on the walk back to his trailer and disagreed about how the next few minutes should go. I was telling him that if his brother had stolen my vehicle, I was going to beat his ass for it. His argument was that he shouldn't suffer from his brother's actions. My response was that because he had chosen to run, he was responsible for everything that went down after that. We got back to find the old Isuzu Trooper exactly where and how I had left it. I'm not sure which one of us was more relieved. I put him in the back seat, shackled him to the floor, and was about to leave. The front door of the trailer was standing wide open either from where I had busted in or, more than likely, where Fatty had busted out. Skinny asked me to please shut and lock his front door so the neighbors wouldn't rob him blind. I refused, but he promised to behave on the long trip to jail if I did it for him. So, I stomped up the steps to help him out.

I stepped inside to grab the door handle and could not believe what I was looking at. I was so stunned that it took me a few seconds to react. Fatty was standing in the kitchen, almost exactly where I had left him. He had taken the time to put a shirt and shoes on while I was gone. Logic dictated that he should have been long gone by then, and I hadn't even remotely considered going back in to look for him. I drew my wet gun and yelled "Get on the fucking floor!" I was in no mood to fight this guy and he knew it. He complied and I handcuffed him with no issues. That was a good thing, because I figured the odds of that Glock firing a single round at the time were pretty low, but he couldn't have known that. As I was walking him out, I asked him, "What are you still doing in here, dumbass? Why didn't you run?" I didn't know what sort of an answer to expect, but he said, "I'm fat, man, where am I gonna run to?" I reminded him that my truck was running outside, and he said, "No way I'm stealing a cop car, man." I guess that it's important to note that anyone who can make an arrest are generally referred to as "cops" by these people.

I walked him out to the truck, opened the door, and his brother was as stunned as I was to see him. Skinny said, "What the fuck were you still doing in there, man?" I didn't even give him time to reply when I said, "I just asked him the same damn question, bro."

Important note #1: I did not repent as promised. Important note #2: The Glock worked fine after I cleaned it up and replaced the rounds . I owned it for several more years before selling it.

    I hate seeing "missing" posts on social media that aren't sanctioned by law enforcement. Most of them even say some bullshit like "the police won't help us," or "the cops don't care." This is never the case. The police just know that she isn't actually missing and families don't like to hear the truth. I, however, do not mind telling them.

SKINNY & FATTY 2

Over a year had passed and I was now working for a larger company. I was the new guy there, but they kept me busy because I had much more experience than any of the other employees at the time. As fate would have it, this company had bailed Fatty and Skinny out of jail after I had finally caught up to them at my last job. So, it was no big surprise to me when I learned that they skipped court again. I had the advantage of knowing them pretty well, knowing where they lived, and knowing the surrounding area. Armed with that information, I certainly wasn't going to go back down there alone. But the brothers weren't going to be caught so easily this time. They had abandoned their trailer, and it had been quickly rendered unlivable. The neighbors had stripped it of all its copper wiring and appliances. The heating system was even gone, along with the light sockets and electrical outlets. If it had been worth a dollar, it was stolen and gone. Skinny and Fatty were in the wind again

A deputy sheriff from a neighboring county called me one evening and asked if I wanted to go on an adventure. He had received a tip on the brothers from a tipster whom he had worked with before, and he wanted to follow up on it. He knew that I had been looking for them, so he thought I might want to help him out. His information was that the dipshit duo was supposed to be camping in a very remote part of the county. When I say remote, I mean that it was supposed to be a place you had to walk three or four miles in to. It would be dark soon, so we dressed for a night hike, got our equipment together and headed out. He parked his cruiser at a local store and rode with me in my lifted SUV. We got as far as we could up the steep mountain trail and eventually had to hide my vehicle in the woods. We camouflaged it with some brush and sticks and started our hike.

We weren't sure how far we had to go, only that the campsite was supposed to be near an apple orchard at the top of the mountain. The deputy told me that there was rumored to be more than one apple orchard up there, which was going to make this even more difficult. He also told me that the only way up here was by ATV or on foot. It was his understanding that there was no access to this mountain by regular vehicle. So, we forged on towards the summit as the sun went down.

It ended up being about a two mile walk before the ground leveled out. It was quite a beautiful area with clearings, wooded areas, and all sorts of vegetation. The small path we had been walking opened up into a larger trail with lots of worn ruts from ATV traffic. It was completely dark now, but we had decent moonlight and only needed our flashlights intermittently when the trails became tree covered. At one point while my flashlight was on, I looked down to see fresh tire tracks. Not ATV tracks, these were from full size truck tires. These trails were narrow, but I could see driving a truck on them if you didn't mind the sides getting scuffed up some. Whoever told the deputy that there was no access to this place was wrong. You couldn't have driven here from where we came in, but there was another way in here somewhere. We followed the tracks.

It wasn't long before we wandered right past an apple orchard. It was on the right side of the trail and looked to be quite large. Just as we were talking about how we might be getting closer, I spotted a light in the distance. It looked to be a few hundred yards on up the trail and off to the right a bit. Someone else was up here, and we were going to drop in for a visit.

We went into silent mode and switched our flashlights off. We decided that we would walk up closer, get a look at what we were dealing with, and make a plan from there. It only took a few minutes before we could see the source of the light. It was dim and coming from inside a red tent. The tent wasn't anything fancy, but it was pretty big. It was tall enough to stand up in and probably would have slept five or six pretty easily. We got as close as we could to see more.

The tent was in a large, flat spot alongside the trail. There were lots of tire tracks around it, as if a truck had been pulling in and out for quite some time. You could easily see where the truck had been parking, but it wasn't there this evening. We couldn't tell if anyone was inside the tent. The light was dim, but I feel like it would have highlighted any movement if there were any. There were three camping chairs by the tent, a fire pit, and beer cans strewn all over. If anyone was in there, they were lying down or asleep. So, we made a plan.

The plan was for both of us to creep up on the tent, unzip the door really quickly, and bust in fast and loud. The way we saw it, this was a win/win situation. If they were in there, we would have them dead to rights. If they weren't in there, it was no harm, no foul. So that's exactly what we did. We crept up to the door, unzipped it, and went in yelling, "Sheriff's Department!" You have to conjure up a really mean look and a larger-than-life profile when you make a move like this. The object is to have cuffs on them before they can even gather their thoughts. You yell really loud, shine the flashlights all around and create mayhem just for a few seconds. I had conjured up one of my meanest looks for this one, but it was all for naught. The tent was empty.

There were three dirty sleeping bags inside, a couple of ashtrays, and plenty of trash. Whoever was staying in this shithole had been staying in it for some time. The interior of the place smelled like fresh dog shit might smell if that dog just happened to also have ass cancer. We jumped outside as quickly as we had jumped in and started making a new plan. It wasn't as if there was a long list of options in this scenario. There was really only one thing that we could have done in this particular situation. Set up an ambush.

It wasn't going to be some sort of elaborate, military type ambush that took a lot of time to plan. It was going to be simple. I mean, we were going to hear them coming from a mile away, so we just sat in their camp chairs and waited. We kept our lights off, kept our voices down and devised a strategy. If they walked up on foot, we would back into the shadows and bust them when they got right beside the tent. If there were three of them, this was the worst-case scenario, because being outnumbered would give at least one of them more of an opportunity to run. We hoped they would arrive in the truck that we knew had been here before. This way, we hit them from both sides the exact second that they shut off the engine. There's nowhere to go in that situation.

We sat there for a while, trading stories, and talking about how long we were willing to sit there on that particular night. After all, we didn't know if they were staying there every night or not. We were both pretty committed after that long hike, but not for an all-nighter. But we didn't have to wait very long. Just as we had hoped, we heard a vehicle off in the distance. It had to be them. There was almost zero chance that someone else was driving up in here tonight. We took our places on either side of the campsite. I had the passenger side, the deputy had the driver side, and the headlights were headed straight for us.

The truck pulled up, idled a few seconds, and the driver killed the engine. It was an old, beat up, single cab pickup truck. The kind of truck you might see three shitheads riding around in on a secluded mountain. The windows were both down and there were three adult male occupants inside. The two by the windows had guns pointed at their temples before they could even open one of their doors. The immediate aroma of body odor and stale beer rolled out of the windows like smoke from a Cheech & Chong movie. It smelled just about as bad as the tent. We had them right where we wanted them.

I saw right away that Fatty was behind the wheel. Skinny was in the middle and they had an unknown buddy on the passenger side. I was yelling, "Everyone's hands on the dash where I can see them," and the deputy was yelling at them from his side as well. I swore to shoot the first person who moved their hands and the two on my side were complying. I jerked the door open and ordered their buddy out of the truck. He was terrified and wouldn't move. He wasn't really resisting, but I think his entire outlook on life had just shifted and he had frozen from fear. I grabbed him by the collar, drug him out of the truck, and threw him onto the ground. I screamed at him not to fucking move, but I knew there was zero chance of this guy being a problem. As he looked up at me, I could see a lifetime of emotional scars in his eyes. Looking back, I find that pretty damn funny. If you are that fragile, you probably shouldn't be riding around with shitheads.

I went straight for Skinny, still yelling at him to keep those hands on that dash or I was going to blow his head off. I quickly drug him out to the ground, and cuffed him. The deputy was still yelling something at Fatty, who had tears rolling down his face. I mean, this grown ass man was power crying. But he hadn't been cuffed yet, so I turn my gun back on him and screamed, "Put your fucking hands on the dash or you are going to get shot!" I had my foot on Skinny and probably yelled that out three or four more times before the deputy finally pulled Fatty out of the truck.

I got Skinny up off the ground to walk him over to the driver's side. But first, I made the third wheel get up and run. I pointed into the woods and told him to run like Forest Gump and never look back. I didn't have to tell him twice. He was out of sight in seconds. Dude is probably still running today. We walked around the truck to see Fatty laying on the ground in the fetal position, bawling his eyes out. If that wasn't bad enough, he had pissed all over himself. "Would you look at this shit," I said. "What kind of hardened criminal are you supposed to be?"

We eventually calmed him down and got him stood up. We learned that he had a change of clothes in the tent, so we let him clean up and put dry clothes on. I wouldn't have done that if I didn't have to put him in my vehicle. There was still no chance of him resisting, because he was too traumatized to even talk to us for several minutes. I should have made him walk all the way back in his pissy pants and let him change there, but I was ready to be done with these two idiots. We handcuffed them together, and I hooked a set of leg shackles to the chain to work as a makeshift leash. The deputy led, they followed, and I trailed with my two new fugitives in front of me like I was walking the neighbor's dogs.

It was a long and slow walk back down the mountain, so there was plenty of time for conversation. Usually, I spend my time with fugitives telling them to shut the fuck up, but I'm glad I let these two have a conversation. After all, this was the second time I had arrested them and the second time they were going to ride with me. We had a sacred bond. Fatty had finally started talking a little, so I asked him why he was crying like a little bitch back there. It turns out that while I was screaming at him to put his hands on the dash, the deputy was screaming at him to put his hands behind his head. This was a detail that we hadn't planned for, and during the excitement, I hadn't even noticed. Neither had the deputy. So this dipshit had a gun in his left ear with instructions to put his hands behind his head, and a gun in his right ear telling him to put his hands on the dash. Both of us were threatening to blow his head off if he didn't comply, so he was in quite the quandary. "I just didn't know which one of you motherfuckers was going to kill me first," he said, still crying a little bit. I know there should probably be some sort of moral here about "people's feelings" or "proper planning," but this isn't a Lifetime movie, it's the real world. Fuck Fatty and his feelings.

The family started calling immediately about this one, demanding that I take it off of Facebook. I told them that I do not remove these until the defendant is in custody. It wasn't long until they got their wish.

CRACK BABY

We were pretty sure this guy was staying in this particular motel. We had taken two calls in the last hour from people looking for the reward. Neither of them knew the room number, but both had described an old blue Chevrolet Corsica with plastic taped where the back window used to be. You would be surprised how many shitheads drive cars with trash bags taped into the back window. I mean, what the hell are these people doing to get all these back windows busted out? Anyway, we saw the car as soon as we pulled up. Bobby watched the car while I went to the front desk in the office.

The managers knew me well. I don't think they knew my name, but they absolutely knew me by sight. More importantly, they knew to give me a room key if I asked for one, because they didn't want their doors torn off. I have a reputation of destroying doors in this business, but that's another story. The little foreign couple told me what room the owners of the blue Chevy were staying in and gave me the door key. They, of course, followed me out to watch the show.

We knew this place all too well. There were no back doors, and only a small window in the bathroom. The dude we were looking for was huge and wouldn't possibly fit through that, so we both went to the front door. There was no reason to knock and no reason to play games. The thing to do here was simply unlock the door and walk inside. This is a two-sided coin. The advantage is that you catch them off guard. The disadvantage is that you catch them off guard. (Yes, you read that right.) If you catch them lying in bed, you have them right where you want them. If you catch them loading up guns, it's an entirely different story. So, you have to be prepared for either and anything in between. Either way, you always clearly yell out "bail enforcement" a few times so they don't think this is some kind of robbery. That's exactly what we did.

Upon walking in, guns out, there was a skinny woman standing directly in front of me, but back where the bathroom sink and mirror were. She was clearly a drug addict in really bad shape, and likely high as hell right now. That made her unpredictable. There was an infant lying on the bed and wrapped in a few small blankets. Yelling "freeze" had zero effect on this mouthy bitch. She immediately started bouncing around and screaming at us to get the fuck out of her room. She was extremely over animated and I knew she was only acting like this to warn the fugitive who I was certain was hiding in the bathroom. She was screaming, "They got guns pointed at my baby," at the top of her lungs while I was screaming at him to come out of that bathroom. No one was pointing a gun at her baby.

All of this happened in a matter of seconds, and I wanted this guy out of that bathroom fast. The room was small and Bobby was behind me in the doorway. There was nowhere else to be, so he had to holster his weapon. I was in the only line of fire he had, so his gun was currently of no use to him. Because time was my top priority at that moment, I tried to move straight through the crazy woman and get to that bathroom door. Before I moved a few feet, he stepped out with his hands up. The crack head grabbed the baby and jumped up on the bed, screaming at big man to shoot me. His hands were up, but I was now dealing with total bedlam in this tiny room. The fact that she was telling him to shoot me told me that there was likely a gun in there somewhere. I had no time left. Bobby and I both moved toward my guy when the unthinkable happened. That bitch threw her baby at me.

Now, I don't know if you have ever had a baby thrown at you before, but it's very off-putting. I have heard that women in Europe will throw their babies at tourists while their older kids will steal your wallet and jewelry, but this wasn't Europe. This was a shitty motel room in West Virginia. I would like to add that I feel like anyone who has a baby hurled at them is going to stop whatever they are doing and try to catch said baby. And that's exactly what I did.

I cannot describe to you the pressure involved when it comes to catching a baby. It's probably akin to a fourth down Super Bowl pass when the entire game is on the line. What I can tell you is that the whole catching process is more complicated when you have a .357 Glock in your baby-catching hand. It's even further complicated when a giant fugitive the size of an NFL linebacker plows right through you during the catch. Bobby went for the baby as well, but I was closer and clearly the target to begin with. After all, if you're gonna throw a baby, you want to throw it at the guy with the gun. Against all odds, and while being knocked to the ground, I caught that baby. It wasn't a pretty catch, but it was a catch by any NFL standards. My knee might have hit the carpet just before I rolled, but I had complete baby control before I was down. My gun flew one way,

Bobby flew the other, and dude disappeared into the night.

Hindsight being 20/20 and all, I should have never caught that baby. I can guarantee you, however, that I will never catch another one. That goes double if it's a crack baby. Triple if it's a motel crack baby. Don't send me any nasty emails about this chapter, either, because I don't want to hear it. We all know that if a baby has a mother that's willing to throw it to save her crack dealer, it's probably not going to grow up and be president or anything. That's assuming that it grows up at all.

Let's get back to the motel room. I grabbed my gun and tried to return the baby to mother of the year. Bobby had already chased the fugitive across the road and I wanted to join him, but this bitch wouldn't take her baby back. She actually threw her arms up, backed away, and refused to take it. I don't blame her. I mean, who wants a crack baby? This was just another devious move designed to slow me down, so I just tossed it back on the bed and hauled ass. Needless to say, our guy was long gone.

Baby throwing incident aside, chasing this guy proved to be pretty eventful before it was all over. We arrested a guy once who was pretending to be this same fugitive, and was even carrying his identification. Think about that for a moment. This guy had warrants of his own and was trying to avoid the law by pretending to be someone else with warrants. In the end, he went to jail without providing us any information about the actual guy we were looking for.

The fugitive's older son was killed in a terrible ATV accident some months later. He was flying through town on it with no helmet and was hit by a car. All sorts of law enforcement monitored the funeral, but good old dad didn't show. His other son ended up in prison after also running from the law for a long period of time. Anyhow, dude was finally arrested somewhere in Texas by local police.

Say what you will about his girlfriend, but throwing that crack baby earned him several months of freedom. It was a bold move that paid off. But if you learn only one thing from this story, let it be this. If anyone ever throws a crack baby at you, swat it to the floor.

▓▓▓▓ threatened to come and kick my ass if I posted him on social media. If you see him out pawning his grandmother's TV, please tell him that I will be at my office from 8 - 4 all week.

This all started with a friendly phone call to remind this guy about his court date. He immediately told me that he wouldn't be there and said that "you better not put me on the internet unless you want your ass whipped." I couldn't post this fast enough. We ended up finding him hiding behind a couch.

WHORE DEMOGRAPHICS 101

I want to begin this story by getting one thing out into the open. I cannot stand whores. I have arrested women for just about every crime you can imagine, but whores are by far the worst. They are the nastiest people on earth, and there's not a pair of gloves out there thick enough to make me feel comfortable touching them. As far as I'm concerned, they might as well have roaches crawling out of their asses, because that's how I see them. I would rather fight two grown men than arrest one whore. I will probably get a pile of emails over this chapter, but I don't care. You can live your life as politically correct as you want, but you aren't going to drag me down with you. If a woman has sex with random men for money, she's a whore. It's even in the Bible 14 times. Look it up.

Also, as we approach this subject, it's very important for you to know and understand your basic whore demographics. This isn't something that you learn in school, so let me explain it to you. Like in any other profession, there are always very different levels of employment. The same goes with whores. You may live in a big city someplace where whores work at fancy escort services. The whores employed at those places often appear very attractive, clean, and even hold down respectable jobs on the side. They also generally charge high prices and only sleep with fancy businessmen types. I have never had to arrest one of those whores, but I'm sure it's a real pleasure as far as whores go. The ones that you generally encounter in the Appalachian Mountains are much different. They are skinny drug addicts, covered in open sores, and have very few teeth. They are also in a constant state of tweaking out. This means that they won't hold still, they won't listen to reason, and they won't ever shut the fuck up. That's the kind of whore I was going to arrest today.

This particular whore happened to own her own mobile home, so I didn't anticipate that she was going to be very difficult to find. It goes without saying that the place was left to her by a family member or she would be living out on the streets with all the other whores. She lived several miles from any town and way up a dirt road, so I certainly wasn't looking forward to the drive. But I wasn't going to complain about it. I mean, I was hoping to only make the drive once. Imagine commuting back and forth when you are a whore trying to do whore stuff. It must have been exhausting. Anyway, I just remember hoping that she would be home on this particular day. I don't know what a whore's hours are, but you have to imagine that they are fairly flexible.

My buddy, Ron, rode with me for this arrest. Ron wasn't an actual agent, but he was dependable and always up for a road trip or an adventure. We found the place easily, and the front door was standing wide open as we drove by. It was a nasty place that didn't even look fit for a human to live in. Perfect for a whore. The front yard was mostly bare dirt, strewn with broken down cars, car parts, and scattered trash. We drove past the place, found a wide spot by the road, and put on our gloves and vests. The plan was to head back, pull in quickly, and waste no time going through that open front door. And that's just what we did.

Five seconds couldn't have passed between pulling in and getting to the front door, yet we were that quickly met in the doorway by a rough looking male character. He was skinny, pale, and had a greasy mullet haircut straight out of 1986. That was also about the last time that this dude had taken a shower. He wasn't wearing a shirt and you could count every rib that he had. He was also sporting one of those redneck tans. You know, the kind of tan we would all like to get for the summer, but we can't because we have jobs. But his most outstanding characteristic was his tooth. Yes, tooth, as in singular. He only had the one and it was something to behold. It was a top tooth, and one of what used to be the original pair that would have stood right in the center. All of the other teeth were long gone, leaving this one lone fang in that nasty mouth to fend for itself. I imagined that corn on the cobb hadn't been on his menu for many years. At first glance, it appeared to be an extra-long tooth as well. But in reality, it was probably no longer than yours and mine, but his gums had receded so far into his head that you could see the entire damn thing. It was also mostly brown with a little yellow, indicating that it probably didn't have much time left before it ended up wherever the hell all the others had gone. And this guy tried to block me from coming through the doorway.

I saw our whore standing on the other side of the room and informed them both that I was there to take her to jail. Saying that she looked like death is an understatement. She actually looked as if she had already been dead for several days and no one had given her the bad news yet. I made it clear that I didn't want any trouble and the best way to do this would be to simply give up peacefully. They both instantly started begging me not to take her, as if this were some sort of negotiation and maybe I would just come back another day when it was more convenient for them. You would be surprised how often people do that. I made it clear that we were taking care of this right here and right now. That's when old "long in the tooth" tried to get tough with me. He loudly proclaimed that I wasn't coming into the house and that I needed to "get the fuck off his property!" I made one final appeal to her, told him I was coming in whether he liked it or not, and told them both to keep their hands where I could see them. He stood his ground, grabbed both sides of the door frame and yelled, "Run, baby!" And down the hallway she went.

I went straight through the doorway like that dumbass had never even been standing there blocking me. I have had more trouble negotiating a set of those hippie hanging bead doors than I had getting past him. I slung him across the room like the little bitch he was and went after her. I hit the hallway just as she went out the back door, which put me about two seconds behind her. I had no idea what was awaiting me as I bolted through that rear threshold in a dead run, but it was like I had jumped through some sort of science fiction portal into another world.

When one runs out a back door, there are several things that one might expect to see. Maybe a small porch. Possibly some woods or a back yard of some sort. I jumped into none of the above. Instead, I found myself standing waist deep in garbage. The entire back yard was trash. There were hundreds, if not thousands, of garbage bags, most torn open by animals and spread out across the entire property. To say that I was pissed off would not begin to describe my attitude. Our whore was right in the middle of it as well, trying her best to make a getaway. But there was no easy exit here. This mess was impossible to run in, and that went for both of us. To make it worse on her, Ron had made his way around back by now and was trying to block her exit from this makeshift dump. Both of us were hopping over and through that trash at about half the speed of smell, so the slow-motion chase was on. What a picture it must have been. I was trying to catch her, she was trying every avenue she could find to escape, and Ron was circling the dump blocking her path every time she changed direction. On top of that, Snaggle Tooth was trying to block Ron's progress so she could get away. This was beyond nasty and I was furious.

We were in that hepatitis-ridden maze from hell for several minutes before I finally got my hands on her. I'm not sure what was worse, jumping around in that diseased ball pit or having to actually touch her. She fought with me but I drug her out by her hair like a caveman might have drug a dead deer. Snaggle was trying to get at me, yelling that I was killing her, but Ron kept him pretty much at bay while I got her handcuffed. It wasn't like he was a major threat, but he was certainly impeding this whole process. I screamed at him to "back the fuck up or I swear I will beat your ass when I get her in my truck." He backed off a bit at first while we walked her around the house towards my vehicle. But the closer we got, the more agitated he became. Ron tried to run block while I loaded her up, but he kept pushing through and trying to grab me. I had her half in the truck and had to threaten him with a beating just to buy enough time to get her seatbelted in. I got her situated, Ron walked to the passenger side, and that's when old Snaggle fucked up for the last time. He physically jumped on me.

He tackled me from behind as I was trying to get into the driver seat, wrapped me up like a monkey, and screamed "Run baby, I got him!" But he didn't have me. And she couldn't run no matter how hard she tried. She was cuffed behind her back, in a seatbelt, and both doors were child locked. I peeled him off of me and literally threw him to the ground like a doll, screaming at him to "back the fuck up." I just wanted to leave and he wasn't going to let me. He complied for a second and I told him to keep his distance as I was trying to back up towards my vehicle. But just as I was about to get in, he came at me again. I decided that this was going to be the last time.

Meth heads are quick. They are also small, light, and really hard to hurt. They actually have many advantages in a fight. But they also have one huge disadvantage. They're stupid. Three of this guy couldn't have hurt me, but he was certainly keeping me from leaving and creating a dangerous situation. As he charged me this time, I hit him with my fist, square in the face. I hit him as hard as I could. I tried to punch straight through his face and out the back of his head. I only hit him once, but I hit him for blocking that door. I hit him for telling her to run. I hit him for tackling me. But most of all, I hit him for all that goddamn trash I had been trampling around in. He fell like a sack of gravel. Ron was back out of the vehicle and no more than three feet away when this all went down. Snaggle had landed half on his back and half in the fetal position, all twisted up and unconscious. But what stood out was the blood pouring out of his mouth and nose. I guess I had landed that punch dead center. "Get in the fucking truck," I told Ron, who was visibly shaken from the sight. He said, "Dude, I think you killed him!" I knew he wasn't dead. I could see that he was breathing, and besides, you can't kill a meth head. They have more lives than a cat. You need a silver bullet to kill a werewolf and it takes a wooden stake through the heart for a vampire, but who knows what it takes to kill a meth head. Maybe a job application? Anyhow, before I could even explain this all to Ron, Snaggle started to move again. I told Ron to get his ass in the truck so we could get the hell out of there.

Because I had pulled in so quickly, I had to make a three- or four-point turn to get out of the yard. Not an easy task when you are in a hurry, dodging trash, car engines, and trying to outrun a meth head. Before I could get turned around, Snaggle was already up and pounding on Ron's window.

He had his bloody face pressed against the glass, screaming some shit I couldn't understand. It was like he was an extra in a bad zombie movie, yelling "brains!" I got my vehicle into drive and ripped out of there as hard as I could. That's about when Ron started laughing.

Ron was doubled over in the passenger seat, laughing so hard that he had tears in his eyes. I, however, was not seeing the humor in any of this. It was going to take me several miles and a few beers to get over the last 15 minutes and I couldn't figure out what he had found so damn funny. Eventually, when he was able to talk, he pointed into the back seat and said, "Listen to that bitch!" I had been so focused on getting the truck turned around that I had been ignoring the fact that our whore was yelling and crying in the back seat. When I finally tuned her back in, I heard her crying over and over, "You knocked his tooth out, you knocked his tooth out!" She just kept on saying it and Ron just kept on laughing. She cried all the way to the jail and Ron just kept on laughing. Me, I just wanted a hot shower and an HIV test.

A short stay in jail wasn't going to keep these two apart. They stayed together for several years, each getting arrested for domestic violence fairly regularly. I would see her walking through town regularly when the weather was whore friendly. It was business as usual with them until one of their fights escalated while they were visiting her mother on Valentine's Day. I'm not sure what they were fighting about, but she shot old Snaggle in the balls with a pistol. What could possibly be more romantic than that? But don't worry, just like that final tooth, he was resilient and hung in there. Sometimes, over a cold beer, Ron will start laughing out of nowhere and say, "Remember the time you knocked that dude's tooth out?"

❦ ❦ ❦

HIM: I went to jail last night for domestic battery.

ME: Dude, it was Valentine's Day!

HIM: I know. It was a bad one.

ME: My computer says I bonded you out on a domestic last Valentine's Day!

HIM: Yeah, it's been two bad ones in a row.

Over the years, I have come across many hand written signs. I wish that I had started taking pictures of them before I did, but I still have several that I want to share with you. This one was clearly the work of decent neighbor who was sick of the shithead traffic on their road.

TWO PADLOCKS & A HOUSE FIRE

B ill and I were once headed two states away looking for a female who had fled the jurisdiction. Someone in her family had assured us that she was at this particular address with her boyfriend, so we had left out early that morning to check it out. When we arrived, there were no vehicles in the driveway, so we parked up the road in a spot where we could clearly see the area. This is always a difficult call to make. We didn't have any information besides that address, so it was pure guesswork on how to proceed from there. We could have gone and knocked on the door immediately. But if someone had been home and she was out, we would have never caught her there again. She might have also answered the door herself, but you never know. We could also have shown her picture to neighbors, but that presents its own risks. You never know if they are friends who might call and warn her. The neighbors could also hate them and give you all sorts of valuable information. Every case and every neighborhood is different, so sometimes it's best to sit back and watch for a bit before you decide how to proceed.

A few hours into the surveillance, a man arrived at the house in an older model, beat up car. He got out of the car and walked inside carrying a few small bags and a power drill. He wasn't inside very long before he came back outside with same stuff. What he did next took us a few minutes to figure out, but when we did, it raised several questions. He was installing hasps and padlocks on the outside of both doors to the home. Anyone with any common sense would agree that this was odd. We watched him finish and leave the area, so we followed him. There was no reason to watch this place right now, because no one was going to get in or out of that house without him and his keys.

This guy led us all over the county. He was just running errands, stopping at other homes, and seemed to be driving around aimlessly. I was picking my brain trying to figure out why dude would have put locks on the outside of the house like he did and I eventually came to a conclusion. It was a guess really, but I thought that someone may have told him we were coming today and that he may have locked our girl inside the house. After all, if we had shown up to see padlocks on the outside of the house, it would have appeared that no one would have been inside. It was a long shot, but nothing else made sense. If I was right, dude was smarter than he looked. So, I decided to call the family member that had given us the address to begin with.

Our tipster said that she was going to call the defendant on the phone and try to learn where she was without raising suspicion. It wasn't very long before they returned my call. The tipster said "This is gonna sound weird, but she said that she is locked up in her house today." Little did she know that this didn't sound weird at all to us right now. I was right. We left dude to whatever the hell he was doing and headed back towards her house. This was a unique situation, to say the least.

When we got there, we decided to park a few blocks away, walk in, and go ahead and speak to some neighbors. We felt sure that she was in there, but when it comes to breaking a door down, you want to be positive. Especially when you are in another state. We found a neighbor who recognized her immediately and confirmed that she lived there. It was a risky move, but we decided to make entry into the home.

We went to the back door, out of sight from most of the neighbors. We certainly weren't going to demolish a front door for the entire world to see. Bill was checking out the lock and the door to see how difficult it was going to be to get into. I started walking around the house and looking into windows. I tried to look nonchalant, but that's tough to do when all your actions say "peeping Tom." I was sneaking a look into the laundry room window when I saw her. Actually, we saw each other at the same time. Of course, she screamed.

I identified myself, but she was still yelling at me to get off the property or she was calling the police. I knew that she was going to do no such thing. She knew damn well who I was and she knew that she had warrants. What she did do was call her boyfriend, screaming at him to come and help her. I ran around the house and quickly told Bill to "get in there right now!" We needed to grab her up before the boyfriend got back and made this a bigger scene than it had to be. We knew he wasn't very far away when we had left him, so the race was on.

That door was short work for Bill. There was the outside lock, plus the regular locks, but he was through the threshold inside of 30 seconds. I followed him in, and she was running and screaming through the house like we were there to kill her. We had her cuffed in no time and had to drag her outside, kicking and screaming. I had Bill hold her out back while I ran to get the vehicle. I drove it straight through the yard and right out back to where they were. It took both of us to get her screaming ass into the car and this had to look like an abduction to anyone who might have witnessed it. We were loaded up and gone in no time, and I was pretty sure no one had seen us. But I wasn't positive.

It had been such a fiasco that we decided to call 911 and report the incident ourselves. We let them know who we were, what we were driving, and exactly what we were doing. They seemed pretty much uninterested, took our information, and that was that. A few miles down the road, we passed the boyfriend and I thought it would be funny to point that out to her. I mean, she was already crying, so I said, "wave bye to him!" But the weird shit wasn't over yet.

Before long, Bill got her mostly calmed down and talking a bit and it didn't take any time at all before she started getting mouthy. She was talking nonsense about how we "almost never found her," and how she "almost got away forever." I told her that made no sense coming from someone in handcuffs. She asked me,

"What if you hadn't been able to kick that door in? What would you have done then?" I again told her that none of this made any sense because we, in fact, did kick that door in. But she kept on. "Well, I want to know what you would have done if you couldn't have got into the house." I thought about it for a second and answered her. "I would have probably set the house on fire and just stood around outside waiting for you jump out a window." Suddenly, it was as if I had punched her in the face. She started screaming bloody murder and yelling out shit we couldn't even understand. It was so bad that we had to pull the car over into a store parking lot. Bill asked me to get us a cold drink while he tried to calm her down, so I went inside to get away from it all for a few minutes.

By the time that I came out of the store, she was in the back seat crying uncontrollably, but no longer screaming. Bill was standing outside the car trying not to laugh about something. He closed her door and I could see that he had something to tell me. It turned out that her two children had died in a house fire a few months ago. It also turned out that losing her home was one of the reasons that she had fled the state. She thought that I knew about that fire, and that I was just being mean to her when I had answered her earlier. Bill assured her that neither of us had any idea and that it was all an unfortunate misunderstanding. So, we all got back on the road home, enjoying cold drinks.

Her and Bill talked a little on the trip back, but it was a few hours before she would speak to me again. At one point she asked me, "Do you promise that you didn't know about my kids?" I assured her that I did not. Remember, we were not dealing with a rational person here. I mean, her children had recently died in a house fire, and she had just allowed her boyfriend to padlock her inside her home. At some point, she asked Bill, "Is he lying to me? Did he know about the fire?" Bill told her again that I did not, and he should have left it at that. But if you read my first book, you know that Bill is an asshole. If you didn't read it, you will know it now. "Don't get me wrong," he told her, "He would have said it anyway. He fucking hates kids." And the screaming started all over again.

I would like to tell you that I was looking for Joe, but I wasn't. That did not, however, keep me from asking for him anyway. It turned out that Joe was the previous tenant and hadn't left a change of address with the local drug crowd. The new tenants had warrants, so they ended up wishing that I really had been looking for Joe.

HARRY & BO

I was in the courthouse on business one day at the same time that one of my bail bond clients happened to be on trial. He had been accused of breaking into a convenience store and stealing several items. Are you familiar with those game consoles where you insert a quarter in an attempt to slide the other quarters off the ledge? Well, he was also accused of stealing all of the quarters from one of those machines. The prosecution alleged that he had put all those quarters into a trash bag along with his other newfound booty and carried it home. The prosecution had a witness, who also happened to be one of my clients, so I wanted to drop in and see how it was going.

It's important to note that I rarely attend court with these folks. Sometimes I may go to the courthouse just long enough to make sure that the defendant appears, but there is never a real reason to attend the trial. But this one was different. The defendant and the witness were both very unique and well-known members of the local criminal element. The two of them on opposite sides in a courtroom could be nothing short of entertaining.

The defendant, Harry, was a local badass. I never knew for sure if he was an expert in some form of martial arts, but that was the local rumor. I did see him kick a guy in the face once at a local pool hall. After he knocked the guy out, Harry did a little "show off" dance, spinning and kicking as if he were in a Bruce Lee movie. It looked legit to the locals, but I knew that it could have just as easily been rehearsed and the only move he knew. Either way, he had a reputation for kicking ass and most folks were afraid of him. He and I got along very well, but that was mostly because I kept him out of jail. Remember the guy he kicked in the face? Just before he did it, Harry walked over to where my friends and I were playing pool and asked if the guy was with us. Harry was going to give the guy a pass if he had been. Anyway, I said no and the dude got knocked out.

The witness, Bo, was a complete idiot with the reputation of being a little bitch. So much so, that I could not believe it when I heard he was testifying against Harry. Local law enforcement and I all figured that this case would never even make it to trial. We expected Harry to beat Bo half to death or at least scare him to the point that he retracted his statement. They lived in the same mobile home park, with just a few empty lots between them, and just across the road from the store that had been broken into. How Bo avoided a beating before trial will always remain a mystery, but here we were.

The prosecution alleged that Harry had crossed the road with the trash bag of coins and ripped it open while trying to drag it over the guard rail. Then, they said, he picked up as many as he could, filled part of the bag, and made a few trips back and forth to his trailer with his winnings. The state police had taken a written statement from Bo to the same effect. They called Bo to the stand, and it all went to shit from there.

PROSECUTOR: How many quarters would you say fell to the ground?

BO: I have no idea.

PROSECUTOR: Well, was it 25, 50, 100, or 1,000? Just give me an estimate.

BO: Sir, I have no idea.

PROSECUTOR: You can't even give me an estimate?

BO: No, but it was a bunch.

PROSECUTOR: How do you know it was a bunch?

BO: Because of the chinging sounds.

PROSECUTOR: Chinging sounds? What do you mean?

BO: You know, when the quarters fell in the road. There were a bunch of chings.

PROSECUTOR: Okay then, how many chings did you hear?

BO: (aggravated and loud) I DON'T KNOW!

PROSECUTOR: Can you count, sir?

BO: Kinda.

PROSECUTOR: Kinda? Can you count to ten?

BO: (offended) Yeah, I can count to ten!

PROSECUTOR: Can you count to twenty?

BO: (hesitant) I could probably count to twenty.

PROSECUTOR: Can you count to one hundred?

BO: (ashamed) No, I can't count to one hundred.

So, that line of questioning would prove very important to this case. The prosecutor went on for a bit in an attempt to make the jury believe Bo's statement. I will let you decide for yourselves if they succeeded at that. The prosecutor introduced Bo's written statement to the jury, only to learn that he didn't even write it. It turned out that the trooper had written the statement and Bo had just put an "X" on it for his signature. The prosecutor had not done his homework and this certainly weakened his case. I mean, he had introduced his main piece of evidence as a written statement, and then Bo testified on the stand that he couldn't read or write. But it got even better.

PROSECUTOR: How far do you live away from the defendant?

BO: Two or three hundred feet.

HARRY: (jumping up and screaming) BULLSHIT! He lives over 200 yards from me!

JUDGE: Order in the Court! Sit down sir, and do not interrupt again!

PROSECUTOR: Again, how far do you live away from the defendant?

BO: About two or three hundred feet.

HARRY: (jumping up and screaming again) THAT'S A GODDAMN LIE!

JUDGE: Sit down sir! If you interrupt again, I will have you removed from this courtroom and continue this trial without you!

PROSECUTOR: One more time, sir. How far do you live from the defendant?

BO: (clearly scared to answer, and in a timid voice) Two or three hundred feet.

HARRY: (jumped up and actually took a few steps towards Bo) BULLSHIT! He's a liar!

The judge had clearly had enough of this. One of the two bailiffs had already jumped between the two when the judge ordered Harry to be removed from the courtroom. Harry was not going to go easily and it took both bailiffs to take him out. They drug him out kicking and screaming, but not before he yelled out his last statement that erupted the entire courtroom, including the jury, into laughter. "JUDGE! HE SAID HE CAN'T READ, WRITE, OR COUNT! DO YOU THINK HE CAN FUCKING MEASURE?"

The courtroom turned into a circus. The judge was visibly pissed, and he immediately ordered the jury to do the impossible. He instructed them that they had to disregard that last statement as if it never happened. They were told that they could not weigh that into evidence when they were making their final decision as to guilt or innocence. No human could have ignored or forgot that outburst. Jury duty is generally boring, but this particular group had hit the jackpot.

The trial went on without Harry. His defense attorney cross examined Bo in an effort to discredit him and show the jury that he had a long-lasting feud with Harry. He attempted to make it look like Bo made up the whole story to "get rid" of his nemesis from the mobile home park once and for all. I'm not sure if it was this defense or Harry's outburst that swayed the jury, but they found him not guilty. The prosecutor was furious, but I lay most of the blame on him. He should have interviewed Bo and went over that statement beforehand. That would have changed his entire case, and maybe even lead to a plea, avoiding a trial altogether.

Some months later, Harry died of an overdose in that same mobile home. It was big news in the criminal world and no one in law enforcement was sad to see him go. Bo died not long after in his mobile home, just two or three hundred feet away, or two hundred yards away, depending on who you ask.

Another clear case of a new renter leaving a note for visitors. I wasn't in the building to knock on this door at all, and I somehow resisted the urge to do it anyway.

FUCK YOUR DOOR

Two of us were headed out of town on a fresh tip. I had never met this fugitive before, but a quick look through his file on the way told me everything I needed to know about him. He had spent several years in prison for attempted murder, and was still out on parole when he caught a new misdemeanor charge. Bonding someone on parole is generally pretty safe because the defendant would be looking at real jail time if he missed court. Failure to appear would result in a parole violation, sending them back to prison for the remainder of their original sentence, so they rarely miss under these circumstances. But this guy did miss court because he had bigger problems. While he was out on bond, he tried to rape his female parole officer during what should have been a routine visit. Now, he was in the wind, and we weren't the only ones looking for him.

After reading all of that in the file, I looked at his photo and personal information. I instantly had to do a double take. Could he really be 6' 9" tall and weigh 300 pounds? P.J. was driving and I asked, "Did you see how big this bastard is?" When he told me that he was aware of this, I had to ask another question. "Why are there just two of us going?" This was a four-man job if I had ever seen one. If this gorilla tried to rape his parole officer, he probably wouldn't hesitate snapping his bail bondsman's head back like a Pez dispenser. So, I called ahead and spoke to local law enforcement. They knew who this guy was and agreed to meet us at our destination.

Our tipster had given us good directions, so the place was easy enough to find. It was a filthy mobile home, parked between a few more just like it. The truck that our tipster said he had been driving was parked in the yard. It was after 9 p.m. and pretty dark out, but there were a few street lights illuminating the area. Only one local officer had shown up, but at least it would be three against one if it all went south. P.J. and I went to the front door and the officer guy went to the back door. Never judge or take the back door man for granted. I had learned that the hard way early in my career, and have taught the same lesson to a few others over the years. The back door can often be where all the action is. Fugitives love to bolt out their back doors when someone knocks on their front doors. Can you imagine someone this guy's size running out on you in a panic? But there would be no back yard brawl tonight.

   I knocked on the door. I knocked like a neighbor might knock, not like the police would. Everyone in the criminal world knows the difference, but in case you don't, let me explain. There's a light knock, like you want to borrow a cup of sugar and not alarm anyone inside. Then there's the police knock, which is hard as hell while yelling out bail enforcement really loud. Every case calls for different approaches and sometimes it's admittedly just guesswork, but tonight was a "cup of sugar" kind of night. Not that it really mattered. This guy was meaner than a striped snake and he was probably going to be leery either way. We got no response. There were a few lights on inside but no movement. After several light knocks, I turned it up a little, but still got no response. The neighbors heard the commotion and came outside to see what was going on.

   P.J. walked over to talk to them and show them a photo of the fugitive, who they recognized right away. They told him that he had been in and out of this trailer for weeks, and confirmed that this was indeed his truck in the driveway. They also assured us that he was inside the home with the female resident right now. They told us that the pair had rolled in a few hours ago, and they were both so drunk that they could barely walk. So, now we had two possible scenarios. Were they in there just keeping quiet and ignoring us, or were they drunk and passed out? Whichever it was, we weren't going away. After a brief discussion between the three of us, we decided to break the door down. We generally don't force entry unless we actually see the defendant inside, but this was a little different. This dude was a legit danger to society and wanted by every agency is the area, so we knew that we would be afforded a wide berth on this one.

It was an old mobile home with no storm door, so this was going to be an easy one for me. Everyone got into place, I turned around, and mule-kicked the door as hard as I could. Saying that it came open would be an understatement. The entire door frame dislodged from the home, and the whole assembly opened up in one piece. I had never seen this happen before and was pretty impressed with myself. But there was no time to admire my work, because we all had to enter the home and do a tactical search. That includes flashlights, guns out, and yelling bail enforcement several times. We had them both located in seconds, passed out in bed together.

The neighbor had not been exaggerating. These two must have been on one hell of a drunk today to have slept through all of this. Our fugitive was lying on his stomach, passed out with his face in a pool of his own puke. I mean, I hope it was his own. This was turning out to be much easier than I had guessed that it would. We had already anticipated that this guy would be too big for handcuffs, so we had two sets of leg shackles with us. We put a pair on his ankles and used the other set to cuff his hands behind his back while was he was still unresponsive. We decided to wake up his girlfriend first and get her out of the room. It took some shaking, but we finally got her up and understanding what was going on. I'm sure that being woken up by three guys with guns must have been a shock to her. That proved true, because she quickly turned into a maniac. She started screaming at us to get out of her house and jumping around like a crazy person. Somehow, it became my job to get her into the living room and calmed down, so I tried my best to make that happen.

I pretty much had to wrestle her down the hall, trying to make her understand that this arrest was going to happen whether she liked it or not. I also told her that one of us was local police, and that he would arrest her for harboring a fugitive if she didn't sit down in a chair and behave. That worked for a minute or so. Just about the time that she started to relax, she saw her front door and the fight was on again.

She was pissed. I really needed to be making sure everything was going smoothly back in that bedroom, but instead, I was in here dealing with this shit. After all sorts of screaming back and forth, I grabbed the door frame in an effort to put it back into the empty hole in the wall, but that was an impossible task. I was, however, able to get it to at least look as if it might work again. I made up some bullshit like, "Look, it just needs a few screws in it to be as good as new." I even managed to unlock it and actually swing the door in it's frame a few times. It was actually a time bomb about to blow to pieces, but I finally got her into a chair and calm enough so that I could get back down the hall.

It had been quiet back there, which I imagined could have only been a good thing. By the time I got back down the hall, they already had Andre the Giant in the bathroom, cleaning him up. Nobody wants to transport someone covered in puke if there's a way around it. He was very soft spoken and was giving them no trouble at all, so they even let him get dressed. That's something we rarely do. People say that it's mean, but you want to avoid giving these idiots one extra second to try to fight or get away. It's usually safest to get in, get out, and take them like you found them. The jail will give them clothes and shoes when they get there. Nevertheless, he got dressed without incident, and it was lucky for him, because I doubt the jail had anything in his size.

It was a short walk back out to the vehicle, but it was going to be a rough one. I was the first one out the front door, careful to open it without collapsing what I knew to be nothing but a fragile house of cards. She was standing right in the middle of the room and I didn't want to set her off again. The officer came through, then Andre, followed by P.J. That's when it happened. P.J. tried to pull the door closed behind him as he walked out. But you and I both know that isn't how it went. The door went right past the closed position, kept on swinging, and swung outside to hit the side of the trailer. It was like pulling the last block from the bottom of a Jenga game. The entire assembly, frame and all, fell down the stairs and into the yard. There was now just a huge hole in the side of the trailer where it all used to be. I suddenly found myself running block again.

She came out through the new hole screaming and raising hell again while my partners were trying to shove King Kong into the back seat of an Impala. It was one of those shitty, little 90's models, very different from the older, roomy police cars. That task alone was like an elephant trying to shit into a sock, and I was trying to fend her off while they were doing it. Once he was loaded up, the police officer came over to deal with her while I jumped into the car. Just before we pulled away, P.J. rolled his window down and yelled, "Hey lady, you might want to get somebody to look at that door, I think it might be broken!" We had an eventless ride to jail, leaving that poor officer back there to deal with the fallout.

I'm out I heard the shit u talked to my mom I'll see u one day and I'll show u a tough mf see how much a man u are u POS pussy I seen how nervous u was putting them cuff on me and u had a right to be u have no clue how bad I am all u had to do is just put me in cuff s and not said a thing I understand u was doing your job but there was no call for that I'll run into u one day and it won't be pretty talking all that shit to her and about a man over traffic crap I was trying to go to work when I got pulled over but your have a good day and if u want to see how tough of a man I am I'll gladly meet u somewhere to show u I had no beef twords you till you ran your cock sucker

This message came to me through Facebook messenger the day this guy got out of jail. It was accompanied by several phone calls as well. I replied to the message with several observations about punctuation and spelling. I also took a screenshot and posted it on my own Facebook, which gained an insane amount of attention. The whole thing was confusing, because it was actually Pedro who cuffed him, not me, and Pedro could have eaten this shithead for breakfast. Also, neither one of us had ever spoken to his mother, so we had no clue what this whole rant was really even about.

Pedro was also the agent who transported him to the jail and he cried all the way there. Using his shithead logic, he believed that his civil rights had been violated. He thought that it was unconstitutional for the police to have ever pulled him over, because he was driving to work. Knowing that, the punctuation shouldn't be surprising at all. Also, he never made good on his threats.

MY KIDNAPPER JUST GOT KIDNAPPED

For several reasons, I hesitated even adding the following story to this book. But, in my preface, I promised you folks that this second installment would be a bit more graphic than the last. Besides, if you are still reading after the chapters on whores and crack babies, I'm sure that you can probably handle this one as well.

I want to start by telling you about the defendant. He was charged with over 150 counts of sexual abuse of a minor by a parent or guardian. In West Virginia, you can be charged with this as a parent, uncle, babysitter, or anyone responsible for the care of a child. This guy happened to be the stepfather of the victim. He was also charged with kidnapping, as a result of keeping the victim against their will for some amount of time. It was big news when it all broke. He had been relatively liked in the community and most folks were stunned when he was charged. Due to the terrible details and the nature of the charges, he quickly became the most hated person in the entire area. Some even thought that he might be murdered when he was released on bail. It was a very large bond, so we kept a tight rein on him during his release. We had him check in with us twice weekly, once in person and once by telephone. It went well right up until a few days before trial. He failed to check in and he wasn't at home when I went to check on him. He was in the wind.

The entire community found out when the trial was set to start and he failed to appear. The trial had to be postponed, a warrant was issued for his arrest, and everyone involved was furious. Imagine how many people this affected. A judge, an entire jury, a prosecution team, police officers, expert witnesses, and most importantly, a little girl victim and her family. The pressure was on me to find him, but I would have plenty of help.

Every law enforcement agency in the area was looking for him as hard as I was. It was quite the spectacle. If you were related to this guy, friends with him, or even a neighbor, you had your house searched more than once. State troopers set up random road blocks on random nights, hoping to catch him moving around. Dozens of tips were phoned in and followed up on. He had no money or resources, so everyone agreed that he probably hadn't fled the area. He was very likely somewhere right under our noses.

A few months went by and things calmed down a little with law enforcement. After doing this job long enough, you learn that eventually, these things just seem to work themselves out. I mean, we aren't exactly dealing with the D.B. Coopers of the world here. As the search relaxes, so does the fugitive's actions. They are more apt to become relaxed and make a mistake. Sometimes, they end up in jail one morning for shoplifting a few counties away or grabbed up in a traffic stop. But this guy's end would come in the simple form of a phone call.

The caller told us that he knew for a fact where our guy was hiding and that we could find him there right now. Due to a pretty substantial reward, we had taken several calls similar to this one over the past months, but this one just seemed more legit to me. You can never be right all the time, but over the years you can develop a sense for these things. Legit or not, I loaded up another bail agent and headed that way.

Our destination was several miles up a muddy dirt road. Part of the road was actually a creek. That may be difficult for city folk to imagine, but in southern WV, roads sometimes drop in and out of creek beds. These areas become impassable after heavy rains or snow. They are also not patrolled regularly by the police and make great places to hide out. Cell phones were also of no use to us out there. You have to be careful in these areas because the locals are generally very tight-knit and they are aware the second a vehicle arrives that doesn't belong there. There was no option in this situation but to drive up casually, get out, and make adjustments on the go. But we were about to be making more adjustments than anticipated.

When we pulled in, the defendant was sitting on the porch with two other men and my adrenaline level skyrocketed. He wasn't acting like a fugitive at all. He didn't get up and run, or even hide his face. He knew me well, but didn't know my vehicle, so I pulled my hat down low over my face and started walking towards him. I told my partner not to get out with the shotgun until I got as close I could. He spotted me when I was only about ten steps away. He jumped up out of his chair and yelled, "It's the law!" I immediately drew my Glock, pointed it straight at his face, and told him to get on the ground. My guy was now right behind me with the shotgun on the other two. But this still wasn't going to go smoothly.

One of the guys on the porch had a shotgun of his own. He had it in his hands, but not raised.

Now, our attention was on him. I was moving my pistol back and forth between my fugitive and the guy with the shotgun yelling. "Drop that fucking gun!" I was also telling my partner, "If he raises that weapon, blow his fucking head off!" Dude must have believed it, because he slowly leaned his weapon against the porch railing. I told my partner to move forward and get that shotgun away from him. That's about when it all went south. My fugitive dove over the porch railing and into the front yard.

 I immediately followed, and had my hands on him inside of twenty feet. I took him to the ground while we were both in a dead run, and we crashed into the mud pretty violently. I imagine that his adrenaline was just as high as mine by that time, and that was about to become evident from the fight that was to follow. This guy was a beast for his size. He wasn't any bigger than me, but he was stronger than I could have ever imagined. My partner couldn't help me because he was now holding two shotguns on three other people in the yard, trying to keep them out of this fight. Neither of us knew where the third guy came from, but it really didn't matter. He ended up slinging the newfound shotgun down the driveway so that he could use his own with both hands. It was a sight to see.

My fight was not going well. Every time I thought I had him subdued, he would get away again. As an example of how strong he was, I once had him in a headlock from behind, while sprawled across the hood of a car. Even with all of my weight on him, he slung me off his back and onto the ground. At one point, he turned to run but slipped in the mud. That was the beginning of the end. I kicked him in the center of the shoulder blades while he was on his knees. It was brutal. His head hit the hood of a white Pontiac Fiero that had just pulled in during the fight. Now there was someone else to deal with. But I never saw the driver get out of the car. My guy was now half across the hood of the Fiero, and I was on his back. I only had one cuff on him before he started elbowing me in the side of my head. Don't forget that my partner is still behind me yelling at the others, "Get back or I'll kill every one of you motherfuckers!" They all wanted in on the fight and it was absolute chaos.

I was going to end this once and for all. I couldn't get the cuffs on him, and couldn't allow him to get the best of me here. This was legitimately a life-or-death situation and we needed to get the hell out of here. I grabbed him by the head and started smashing his face on the car hood. It was my only move at the time. I was yelling at him that I wasn't going to stop until he quit fighting, and I kept that promise. I don't know how many times his face hit that hood, but it was enough for the driver's side headlight to start popping up and down. He finally gave out, and I got him cuffed. When I stood him up, I could see that there was blood all over the hood and driver's side fender of that little sports car. Now, we had to get into my truck.

We walked backwards down the driveway with me holding the fugitive with one hand and my pistol in the other. I was using his dumb ass for cover like it was some sort of hostage situation. (For all intents and purposes, it actually was.) There was lots of yelling, "We will kill every motherfucker here," and similar threats, but we finally got into my vehicle safely. I backed down that driveway like a madman, ran over the shotgun that my guy had thrown down the hill, and hauled ass. The headlight on that Fiero was still popping up and down like a strobe light as we sped off.

We weren't in the clear yet. You have to understand the mentality of these people. We had a few miles between us and the main road, and it would have only taken one phone call from those idiots to have that road blocked up ahead somewhere. My SUV was lifted with oversized tires, and I used every inch of clearance that I had leaving that holler. We dropped in and out of those creek beds, wipers on high, slinging water and rocks over the top and behind us. I was driving like we were lead vehicle in a cross-country race. I didn't let up until we were on the pavement. We were relieved to feel like we were in the clear, but our adrenaline was up and the excitement was far from over.

Baby Raper was trying to talk to me and I kept telling him to shut the fuck up. I wasn't interested in anything he had to say right now. I was pretty beat up and my buddy actually thought I needed medical attention. But all I could think of at the time was getting into cell phone service to let the state police know that we had this guy in custody. I knew that they had some sort of new case that they wanted to talk to him about, on top of the charges he had fled. He was by far the most wanted person in the area, and it was going to be big news that we had captured him. Driving along, he kept trying to talk to me. "Gary, you've killed me," he kept repeating, and I just kept telling him to shut the fuck up. I was speeding towards cell service, watching the bars on my phone, and he just kept it up. "Gary, you've killed me." I was tired of telling him to shut his mouth and told him that if he kept it up, I was going to pull over and beat his ass on the side of the road. He was quiet for a bit before he said it again. "Gary, you've killed me. Seriously, I'm going to bleed to death back here." I was way too angry at him to deal with his shit right now. I felt like I was just as beat up as he was and it was a long way to jail, so I decided to pull over and shut him up for the duration of the evening.

I stopped at the next wide spot with every intention of reading him the riot act and shutting his mouth. I got out, opened his door, and that's when I saw it. There was blood everywhere. My old SUV had tan leather seats and now they were completely red. The floor mats were red. The carpet was red. My heart sank and my brain suddenly agreed with him. Holy shit, maybe I have killed him. I asked him where he was bleeding from and he said it was his back. I leaned him forward and immediately saw what was wrong. I'm no doctor, but I'm pretty sure that I shouldn't have been looking directly at his shoulder blade. I mean, the bone itself. It was sticking out of his back and pretty far from where I thought that it probably should have been. Now I had to find a hospital.

I was pushing that old SUV to its limit, heading to the nearest hospital, when one of the troopers called me. They had already heard that I had him in custody and they wanted to talk to him. News travels fast in areas like the one we were in. I told him that they could meet us at the hospital and that he was in no shape to talk right now. The trooper didn't want to hear that. He wanted to know where I was and what hospital I was going to. I told him where I was headed and he hung up. I assumed that this meant he would meet me there. I assumed wrong.

I kept Baby Raper talking and awake while rolling towards the hospital. We weren't far away and I was passing every vehicle on the road with my emergency flashers on. At least, I was until I got to the road block. There were three police cars in the road, blue lights blazing, and officers standing out in the road. I didn't have time for this shit. "I know you think that you're dying back there, but keep your mouth shut," I told him. I wasn't looking forward to explaining to the police why I had a truck full of guns and a bleeding child molester handcuffed in my back seat, but I guessed that I was about to do just that. Wrong again.

This wasn't a DUI stop and this wasn't a random seatbelt check. This was no coincidence at all. I realized when one of the troopers jerked open my back door and scooped Baby Raper out, that this roadblock was set up just for me. I objected for a few seconds, but realized that it wasn't going to get me anywhere. One of the troopers assured me that he would get the medical attention that he needed as they threw him into a police cruiser. Another trooper gave me back my bloody handcuffs and they all just disappeared as quickly as they had shown up. It all went down faster than a well-orchestrated mafia kidnapping. We were left there like it never even happened. Three minutes ago, I was in a frantic, high-speed rush to the hospital. Now, I was sitting quietly in the middle of a dark road with my emergency flashers on for no apparent reason.

I have no idea what happened to Baby Raper that night, but I imagine that it was uncomfortable at best. I would like to say that I didn't care, but I did. Actually, his fate in general meant exactly nothing to me, I was just worried about being sued. Someone has two years to sue you in a situation like that and I spent the entire 24 months worrying about it. I was sort of relieved to learn that he was jailed that night, very relieved when he went to prison for his charges, and EXTREMELY relieved when the two-year statute of limitations expired.

This one is pretty self-explanatory. We see signs like this one quite often, but it's rarely because the resident has a job. It's usually because they are the kind of shitheads that are out stealing and getting high all night. It was afternoon when we were there, so no agents were hurt after we knocked.

JAMES & JAMIE

As you might imagine, there are fugitives from all walks of life. Whether you are a man or a woman makes no difference when you fail to appear in court. Whatever color, creed, or nationality you may be will have no bearing on how we might pursue you. That, of course, goes the same for sexual orientation, sexual preference, or self-identity. This story is about how some over sensitive members of the community reacted to one of my wanted posters. I will use fictitious names for the defendant, but the rest will be 100% accurate.

I remember the day I bonded James out of jail. He called from a holding cell at the courthouse, met all the proper criteria, and I went over to post the bond. The only "catch" was that he didn't have his debit card with him, and I was going to have to run him home to get it. He lived close to our office, so this was no big deal. At least, it shouldn't have been.

When I arrived at the courthouse, I did my paperwork and one of the bailiffs brought James out into the hall, like they had brought a thousand defendants out before him. You never know what someone might look like when they come through those doors. They come out of there just as they were arrested, so I have seen it all and am not easily surprised. It was nothing to see someone emerge with no shoes, no shirt, or both. It wasn't surprising to see black eyes, bloody faces, or even crutches. Some arrests go smoother than others. But James caught my attention when they brought him out.

He was wearing jeans, a women's blouse, and high-heel shoes. He looked as if he had clearly suffered a long night, with his hair all messed up and his mascara running down his face. I admit that it was a bit off-putting, but he was just another client to me. I escorted him out to the old, blue, Ford truck I had at the time, and we headed to his place to get that debit card. Things just got weirder from there.

He lived in a huge old house that had been converted into several apartments. This place was known for criminal activity, and I had made arrests here before. When I pulled into the driveway, he immediately started to panic, crying that he had been robbed. His front door had indeed been kicked in and it was lying in the living room floor. Being the sensitive, caring person that I am, all I could think of to say was, "I hope they didn't get your debit card." He ran inside and immediately started taking inventory. I had to calm him down and tell him that his priority was to find that debit card. He could deal with this mess after I was paid, and I was ready to get the hell out of there. It only took him a few minutes to find it and give it to me. I stepped out onto the porch and called my office to process the payment.

While I was taking care of business, James had answered a phone call that had erupted into yelling. It was extremely heated, and I had to shut him up just to complete my call. When I was finished, I went in to give him his card and some important instructions. You see, he needed to come to my office to complete some paperwork, and the original plan was to do that as soon as he had located his debit card. But now, with his apartment broken into, I was going to let him do it after he had taken care of his business. I was unable to tell him any of this for a moment because he was still yelling on the phone. Keep in mind that I could only hear his half of the conversation.

"No, don't come down here, I've been robbed and have to call the police!"

Unknown caller yelling something....

"That blue truck belongs to my bail bondsman and he's about to leave!"

Unknown caller yelling something….

"No, I'm not fucking him, he's my bail bondsman!"

Unknown caller yelling something….

"Why are you even parked up the street watching me?"

I had heard enough of that shit and started doing some yelling of my own. "Hang that fucking phone up or I'm dragging your ass straight back to jail!" He tried to say a few more words but I snatched the phone out of his hand and decided to yell into that as well. "I am James' bail bondsman, and whoever the fuck you are better stay up the street or wherever the hell you are at," I declared. I told him that if he so much as approached me on my way out that I would stomp his ass into a fine powder, and I hung up the phone. I now had James' full attention. I told him exactly what he needed to do and when he needed to do it. He was, "yes, sir," and "no, sir," the entire time. I left that shit hole, and that should have been the end of it. But you know that it wasn't.

James rolled into my office later that afternoon like a brand-new person. I mean that quite literally. He had showered, fixed his make-up, and put on his best Sunday dress for the occasion. Someone else was on duty at my office, but he insisted on waiting for me to take care of him. At this point, if I hadn't realized that I might have had a new fan, the rest of the office was happy to point it out to me. Taking care of his paperwork was pretty much uneventful until it was time for his mugshot. I did learn that he sometimes went by Jamie, and I noted that in his file. He commented on how lucky it was for him that he had chosen the particular dress that he was wearing today. "This picture is going to be beautiful with the wall color in here," he said. "Whoever chose this color has really good taste." I wasn't about to tell him that it had actually been me, but one of my co-workers was happy to clear that up for him as well. He asked for a copy of his mugshot and I sent him on his way.

It's important to note that I am in no way making fun of James or Jamie. I am simply finding the humor in this story just as I have in every other chapter. You have read along as I made fun of just about everyone. If you laughed when I joked about whores, fish fuckers, and drug addicts, so you can't be offended when I joke about this guy. I mean, you can, but that would make you a narrow-minded simpleton and a hypocrite. It's like going to a comedy show and laughing at the handicapped jokes, laughing at the abortion jokes, and then being offended by a fat joke because you are overweight. Remember, handicapped people are real and you laughed. Abortion is real and you laughed. If you think a fat joke was over the line, then real life might just not be for you. Get mad at me if you want, you already bought my book, so I don't care. I mentioned all of that because it's an integral part of how this story ended up playing out.

James checked in once a week as instructed. But he didn't call in like I told him to, he chose to come into the office and do it in person. His excuse was that he just lived up the street and enjoyed the walk. He was annoying as hell, but we all got used to it. Then, one day, he just stopped coming by. I didn't miss his visits at all, but this was a red flag, so I called him. None of the numbers he had given to us were working anymore. Another red flag. I called the court to learn that his hearing date was coming up and decided to wait and see if this might just work itself out. If he made it to court, our business would be concluded and we could put this all in the rear-view mirror. But he didn't make it to court.

The first thing I did was to pay a visit to his apartment. He didn't live there any longer and the new tenants had no idea who he was. One of the neighbors told me that he was still local, and they had seen him walking around the area frequently. They also told me that his drug problem had gotten much worse and that he was "doing some fucked up shit for money." No one wanted to get any deeper into that conversation. It was time to make a wanted poster for social media.

You guys have seen my controversial wanted posters. They are first and foremost designed for attention. This ensures that they invite plenty of comments and get shared many times. This is how people get located and I figured that this one was going to be fairly easy. Because of the current sensitive nature of about half of our delicate little citizens out there, I even took great care not to make fun of James on the poster. I just wanted to make a joke and make the public aware of exactly who I was looking for. Part of this, of course, is to post a photograph. Photographs, plural, in this case. I went to his

Facebook page and used his own profile pictures for the poster. He had pictures of himself as both James and Jamie on his profile and made no effort to hide who he was. I wasn't going to hide it either. If I wanted to find him, people had to know what he may or may not look like. This harmless, yet factual and informative, wanted poster absolutely exploded on Facebook. Here it is:

I had no idea what a stir this thing was going to cause. The local militant club of LGBT members slapped on their war paint and manned their battle stations. (Can we even say 'manned' anymore?) The phones rang off the hook. The poster was shared hundreds of times per hour. No human could have kept up with the comments. Most opinions were positive or just people joking around, but some were not. Some comments from members of the local trans community and their supporters were downright threatening and violent. To book themselves as a loving and inclusive community, they were the most ruthless and vindictive people that I have ever came across.

I was a busy man a the time this all went down. I also hosted events at a few local businesses, wrote for a local newspaper, and organized art shows in the area. These people called and visited every single place that had anything to do with me, in an attempt to have me 'cancelled.' They showed up with DEI contracts and tried to strong arm these places into not allowing me to work there anymore. They argued that gay and trans people couldn't feel safe in these places unless the owners banned me and signed their very important pieces of paper. They said that they could not tolerate me being uninclusive, and in the same breath, they demanded that I should be unincluded. What a bunch of hypocrites. In the end, no papers were signed and I continued hosting events at every one of those places and more. During all this mess, James saw his wanted poster and called me.

James assured me that he was not on the run and that he had just moved without changing his address. He promised to do whatever I asked of him to fix it, so I asked him to meet me the next morning at my office. Of course, it was Jamie that kept that appointment. Even though I could have arrested him on the spot, I walked him over to the courthouse to see if there was an easier solution. I spoke with the judge and prosecutor, who both agreed to offer him the same deal on this day as they had planned to on the date that he had missed. Everyone got into a room together and the case was settled in minutes.

After so many people got angry about all of this, it was finally over. People were angry at me who didn't even know me. People were angry at me who didn't even know him. People were angry at me because they had made this personal to themselves and their own unresolved issues. As we walked out of the courthouse, James had something pretty telling to say. "You know, I don't know why all those people were mad at you on the internet," he told me. "I think you picked the best two pictures on my entire Facebook page to put on that poster."

ME: You missed court and I had to arrest you the last time I bonded you.

HIM: No sir, you've never arrested me before.

ME: Look at my file buddy, is this your birthday?

HIM: Yeah, but anybody could have used that.

ME: Is this your social security number?

HIM: Yeah, but those get stole all the time, too.

ME: Can you explain this picture I have of you and me standing in front of the jail? You're the one in handcuffs.

HIM: Man, I don't remember that at all.

Na your mom is going to occupy me but this is games you will see me that's a promise and if you won't to go off record I'll gladly beat your bitch ass mf so enjoy that I promise you will see me bitch

Gary Vaughan
Dude...she's in jail. Get over it. NOTHING you say is gonna change that, (or be spelled correctly.)

This aspiring writer went on a Facebook rant after we put his girlfriend in jail. The rest of his threats made about as much sense as this one did. He must have got lost on the way to come and see me.

VACUUM CLEANER

I went to a guy's house once just to talk to him. He had recently missed a court date, but I was able to get it rescheduled for him. I did that because I had bonded him before with no problems and I was giving him the benefit of the doubt on this one. I thought that maybe he just screwed up and he wasn't actually running. The letter that the court had sent him was returned to them and the phone numbers I had were all disconnected. This happens quite a bit, but more often than not, it's just the defendant's lack of keeping his shit together. I figured that I would go talk to him, give him his new court date, and get new phone numbers from him. Since we had a history, I thought I would bend a little and see if I could salvage the relationship. But it was not to be.

He was sitting on the porch with three or four other folks when I pulled up. I wasn't planning to arrest him, so I wasn't in any hurry when I got out of my truck. But that changed quickly. The second that he saw me, he jumped up and ran inside the house. Everyone else on the porch immediately followed him inside. They disappeared like cockroaches after you've switched the light on. The entire scenario was a surprise to me because I didn't come here prepared for any of this. Nonetheless, I ran inside less than ten seconds behind him to see a very odd scene.

Everyone who had filed inside behind him was now sitting in the living room. Three were sitting on the couch and one in a chair. They were just sitting there like they were posing for a photo. All of them were holding very still, sitting straight up, and looking forward. It would have been creepy under any other circumstances, but I knew what was going on. He was hiding in here somewhere and nobody was going to talk to me. It was a terrible plan, but hey, they only had a few seconds to come up with it. I told them I was only going to ask this one time. "Where is he?" Nobody moved. I went into my regular rant about how the police were on the way and I was going to arrest every single one of them for harboring a fugitive. This was, of course, a lie. I have no jurisdiction over anyone but the defendant and there were no police coming.

The four stooges just sat there, almost motionless. Except one. The girl on the far right of the couch, who looked to be the youngest of the crew, was doing something crazy with her eyes. She was using her eyeballs to try and get me to look to my right. She was doing it without moving her head and she wasn't very good at it, but it worked. She was trying to help me, but didn't want any of the others to know it. It was a very small house and there was only one room in the direction she was trying to draw my attention to. So, that's where I went.

There was no door into the room at all. It was connected to the living room by just a large archway. It was a small room with an old washer and dryer in the corner. These appliances must not have been used regularly, because the rest of the room was littered with dirty laundry. What stood out was the one gigantic pile of clothes right in the center. The one that was exactly big enough to have a shithead hiding in it. I knew he was in there. I would have bet on it. So, I decided that I was going to give him one more chance. I was still standing where I could see everyone in the other room.

"I know you are hiding in this pile of laundry," I announced loudly. "I didn't come here to arrest you. I came here with your new court date and to give you another chance to make this right." The four statues in the living room were all now looking at me. Probably because I had picked up an upright vacuum cleaner and was wrapping the cord around the handle while I was talking. "I'm giving you one chance to come out of there and work this out with me," I announced. "If you make me dig you out of this nasty laundry, I'm going to kick your ass and take you to jail." No response again. I raised that vacuum cleaner up onto my shoulder like a baseball bat and said, "Last chance!" But if he was under there, he was standing his ground.

Now I was committed. If he wasn't under there at all, I was really about to look like an idiot. If he was under there, what could he have been thinking? He couldn't possibly have believed that I was just going to go away. Whatever the case, I raised that vacuum cleaner as high as I could and swung it like Babe Ruth aiming for the cheap seats. Before it even came down, I knew he was in there from the look in everyone else's eyes. The eye-roller on the end of the couch actually jumped. The neighbors probably heard him cry out in pain as it smashed down onto his dumb ass. Now he was ready to come out.

I threw the vacuum down as he rolled out onto the floor. I grabbed his arm, put him on his stomach, and he was yelling, "You broke my shoulder!" I put cuffs on him and said, "You can't break your shoulder, dumbass. It's probably just your collar bone." But nothing was broken, he was just a pussy. I led him out to the truck, trying to explain that this didn't have to happen like this. Now, he was begging me to give him that second chance, but that ship had sailed. At least there would be clean clothes in jail.

He was in trouble many more times in the years to come. People like him rarely seem to learn lessons and they never take responsibility for their own actions. He even called my office from jail every now and then, begging for that second chance again. But his bridges were all burned with me and he needed to learn that life didn't always offer a second chance. In the end, I guess that he learned that the hard way, as I learned a few years ago that he died of an overdose.

←→

HER: Why did you tell me that I had to come into your office to make a payment? Other people say that you allow them to pay over the phone.

ME: Because they pay with debit cards, ma'am. You pay with a check.

Wow all u grown ass adults acting like a bunch of elementary School kids all over me... It's cute but very immature, and how much is that reward, hell I may turn myself in an collect it... Gary you know those false statements only puts a smile on your face when your trying to look cool on social media, truth be told all of you sound like a bunch of children on a school bus. My seven-year-old daughter has a better education then you idiot's.. but please don't let me interrupt your stupidity, while you make me famous back home on that simple possession charge, I'ma sip 2 Pina colada, an continue to enjoy my vacation.. look I'ma prey for you guys ok seriously y'all need maturity and Jesus...

This simpleton was commenting on his own wanted poster, trying to act like he was on the beach somewhere. His girlfriend turned him in for the reward, and we arrested him less than 24 hours after he made this post.

She led us right to the ratty mobile home that he was hiding in. He ran when we busted in on him and refused to surrender when we had him surrounded. His dumb ass still wanted to fight after Pedro body slammed him, and he somehow ended up hit in the head with my shotgun during the scuffle. Once he was handcuffed, his entire attitude changed.

He begged over and over for us to give him another chance on the walk back to my truck, but that ship had sailed. He cried all the way to jail. The harder he would cry, the harder Pedro would fuck with him. "I didn't see any beach back there," Pedro told him. The badass that had been on Facebook yesterday was long gone.

I DIDN'T KILL HIM, YOU DID!

B ill and I had spent several days in North Carolina looking for a fugitive. He had fled the area and we had received word about some relatives that he might have been staying with down there. We had watched the relatives for a few days and even searched a few houses before we gave up and came back home empty handed. It's always frustrating when this happens, but it's part of the job. When we got home, we decided to increase the reward money to an amount that would get some real attention. You have to be careful and calculating when you do that. You have to know that the larger the reward is, the more bogus phone calls you are going to get. People will call in with tips that are outdated, information that you already know, or just shit that they made up. The only way to really filter through all that is experience. And those calls started coming in fast.

A few weeks into it, we got a call that we considered solid. The caller told us several pieces of information that we already knew were factual, so that gave more credit to the new information that they had. We were told that our fugitive was staying in North Carolina with an old friend. We also learned that he was planning to come back into WV that very night to go to his grandmothers and pick up the rest of his clothes. The caller even knew what kind of car they were traveling in, and had the NC tag number. The info sounded solid, so we immediately set up a surveillance on his grandmother's home.

We knew the place well. The entire family was shitheads and I had arrested a few people there before. Two of us got dropped off on foot, and hid in the woods across the road where we could see the house and property. It was a large, one level place with several vehicles in the driveway. There was also a large camper in the driveway, set up on blocks with power ran to it. People were coming and going from the home and camper while we were there, so we had to be ready for anything. Two other agents, both with their own vehicle, parked a mile or so up the road in either direction. We were all, of course, keeping each other updated via cell phone. This way, from whichever direction our guy approached, we would have some warning and be able to block him in when he arrived. So now, it was time to just wait.

We didn't have to wait very long. We got a call from one of our guys that the car was on the way in. I told them to follow it, and pull in behind it after about 30 seconds. We were going to need at least that long to get down the bank and across the road. The car pulled in, and the next seconds happened fast. I would have liked to have caught him inside the car, but there was simply not enough time to do that. He and the driver were out of the car and inside the camper within five seconds. They were in there before our backup even pulled in or we could get across the street. So, now, we were going to have to go into the camper.

I went in first. The door was open and I just walked right in. There wasn't much space to move inside there at all. Our guy was right in front of me and I told him to put his hands behind his head. Instead of complying, he charged me. The fight was on right there inside the camper door. I guessed that he was trying to plow past me, unaware that there were three more agents right behind me to catch him. There was zero chance of him getting away, but I had to get him subdued. One of my guys was trying to help me but there was just no room. He was actually standing outside, leaned in and helping me fight this guy. Dude was trying to get away like a wild animal and now, two of his friends came in from the back room. My agent at the door drew his gun on them and ordered them onto the couch. Thank goodness that they complied. I had my hands full and it was about to get worse.

Dude was on his stomach and I was on top of him, trying to choke him out. My guy had a gun on his friends and handed me his pepper spray. I did not want to use in inside these close quarters, but I was out of options. I reached around the front of his face and let him have it. In a few seconds, he had stopped fighting and was begging for water. That's when it got weird. There was a room to my right and a gigantic, obese woman had been standing in that doorway screaming the entire time, but honestly, I was too busy to pay much attention to her. But I was paying attention now, and it's a good thing. She had picked up a floor lamp and was coming straight at my head with it.

I was still on the ground with my fugitive in a head lock when she came at me. If you aren't aware, the bottom of a floor lamp is heavy as hell and could really hurt you. I barely saw her coming down with it in enough time to roll out of the way. It missed my head by millimeters. My fugitive was not so lucky. She hit him square on the top of his skull. She had come in so fast and hard that she fell on top of us as she struck him. If her big ass had landed directly on top of me, I would have likely been dead on the scene. But, thankfully she did not. Without even thinking, I shot a load of pepper spray right up her nose and all over her eyes. It wasn't a well-aimed shot or anything, it's just how we were situated, and it worked out that way. Now I couldn't breathe either and I had to get the hell out of that camper. I rolled off of him and out the door, so I could get some air and the other guys could grab him. But that wasn't going to be the easiest of tasks.

Two of the other agents were trying to drag him out the door, but the big girl was now fighting them like hell with her eyes full of pepper spray. One of my guys dropped a large, steel flashlight during the ruckus and she managed to get a hold of it. She was on her knees in a blind rage, swinging it wildly at my guys. She managed to get a few licks in before they took it away from her. She also managed to hit the fugitive a few times as well. By this time, he was all fucked up. After a few minutes, we had him out in the driveway and everyone else at gunpoint. The crazy woman was yelling, "You fucking killed him," over and over. I wasn't in any position to argue with her at the time, but all I had done was pepper sprayed him.

She's the one that had damn near beat him to death. We threw him into one of our cars and hauled ass while biggun' was still yelling and gasping for breath.

We got down the road a bit and pulled over for some air. Any time that you use pepper spray, it makes for a shitty car ride afterwards. We used that time to check out our own injuries and to determine whether or not our fugitive needed to go to the hospital. We pretty much all agreed that he probably did need medical attention. "Who was that fat, crazy bitch back there, anyway?" I asked him while I was looking at the cut on his head. "That was my sister," he answered. I started to form a plan immediately. I told him that I hated going to the hospital, but I was going to take him anyway. "And while one of these guys is watching you, three of us are going back to arrest your sister," I told him. He clearly had no clue that I wasn't allowed to do that, because he begged me not to. I ended up working out a deal with him. We agreed that he would go to jail instead of the hospital and tell the nurse that he was fine. He had thick hair, so he agreed to wait to get his head looked at until they signed for him and we were gone. In turn, I agreed not to arrest his sister that I wasn't going to arrest in the first place.

This one ran to a beach community in California and also liked to comment on his own wanted posters. He even went as far as to make one of them his Facebook profile picture for a while. He was pretty mouthy on social media and thought that he was bulletproof because he was so far away. He was wrong. People like him get in trouble no matter where they live, and it didn't take long for him to land in jail there. But until he did, I made his mother's life pure hell.

She lived between where I lived and where worked at the time, so I drove by her house at least twice a day. Anytime that I had someone with me, or we were already out hunting someone else, we stopped and searched her house. We knew he wasn't there, but it was a way of applying constant pressure. She would cry nearly every time and swear that she was trying to talk him into turning himself in. She knew that was the only way this was ever going to stop. I imagine that she was probably as happy as I was when he finally got arrested.

DIRTBAG IRONY

Spoiler Alert! Not every story ends with a fugitive in custody at the end of the day. Not every mystery gets solved. This is one of those stories. Every single law enforcement agency in my area had been looking for a high-profile fugitive. Their specific target was not one of my clients, but I was well aware of the hunt. I don't remember what type of charge he had actually fled on, but he was also wanted for questioning in an ongoing murder investigation. The target had been missing for months and was thought to have fled the state, maybe even the country. And then I got an unexpected tip one afternoon.

I was out that day, arresting one of my own defendants. It was a pretty simple arrest that hardly deserves its own story, but it ended with my guy in my custody. My defendant was a low-level drug dealer. The kind you see in movies that hang out on street corners peddling pills to kids. I had actually picked him up in a school zone with a pocket full of drugs. He was wearing baggy pants, an oversized hoodie, and had a brand-new tattoo on his face. He certainly looked the thug part, and he had most of his neighborhood fooled, but I knew better.

There are few things funnier to me than a self-proclaimed bad ass crying like a little girl. I probably enjoy it more than I should. If you think about it, it's like the two of you are forming a special bond. He might have his friends, neighbors, and customers thinking that he's a tough guy, but you and him both know the real truth. On our short ride together, this guy's power crying was giving me a real and unobstructed look at who he really was. The closer we got to our destination, the worse his pleading and crying got. He tried everything that he could think of to keep me from taking him into the jail, but nothing he had to say was going to talk me out of that. At least, I thought there was nothing he could say.

Out of the blue, he mentioned the name of the fugitive that everyone had been looking for. He said that they were cousins and that the fugitive was in town from Texas for a few days. He swore that he could take me right to where he was hiding out if I promised to let him go. It doesn't take a genius to know that someone is his position might have said anything to get set free, but this was different. I knew that the two were from the same neighborhood, so there was a chance that he might actually know something. The wanted fugitive in question was a big deal, so this was at least worth a conversation. Besides, I didn't think this was my decision to make. So, I called one of the officers in charge of the manhunt.

To say that the officer was interested would be an understatement. I turned the car around, and we met in a low traffic area that he had chosen. When I arrived, there were three police cars there waiting for me. It had been a while since there was a decent tip on this fugitive and these guys were clearly ready to act on a new one. They got my guy out of the car and went straight to work on him. The first thing to determine was whether or not he was telling the truth. It was explained to him that if he was lying about this information, he needed to come clean now so we could all move on. It was tough to really know what he knew about the fugitive. On one hand, people like him certainly can't be trusted. On the other, why lead us on a wild goose chase just to piss us all off. But we could talk all day about shithead logic and never figure it out.

The interrogation ended with the decision that Shithead was going to take us to the fugitive. He said that he didn't know the address or street name, but could lead us right there. The plan was for him to hide in the back seat of my car, direct me to the residence, and then I was to relay the address to the police. So that's what we did. Shithead pulled his hood tight, sank down into my back seat, and led me into one of the worst neighborhoods in the area. I was on the phone with the police the entire time. It was a simple and effective plan.

The closer we got to our destination, the more that my guy started freaking out. He was so scared that he could barely even talk, but kept saying that this was going to get him killed. At one point, he even asked me just to take him on to jail. I assured him that if he stayed low and just pointed out the house, that he would be fine. This was all his idea, after all. His actions led me to believe that his info was real and that he was legit scared for his life. I was conveying all of this to law enforcement in real time so that they were armed with the same information that I had. Like I said before, I wasn't in charge of this circus. After driving around a bit, Shithead finally pointed out a house.

I relayed the address to the police and drove on down the block. Shithead had been in full on freak out mode when he had pointed it out and immediately laid down in my back floorboard. "They are gonna fucking kill me," he kept repeating. Let me tell you about the house that he pointed out. It was pretty well kept and nondescript. It was, in fact, the most decent house on the crowded block. But it wasn't this house that had my attention. It was the house next door. The neighbors were having a party. There were probably a dozen people in the front yard next door. They were drinking beer and dancing to loud music coming from one of the several vehicles in the driveway. The hood was up on one of the cars, and a few guys were leaning in like they were working on it. Smoke was rolling out of a few charcoal grills and we could smell the food as we drove by. It was a scene straight out of a gangster rap video that might have been filmed outside of L.A. somewhere. This was going to be interesting at best.

Within a minute or so, the police had the target house surrounded. I turned around and joined them, but hung back a little. Shithead was still in the floorboard getting closer and closer to having a stress-induced stroke. I didn't help much when I laughed and told him to stay down and "hopefully" no one would see him. It was more than just the three police cars here now. It appeared that several more officers had joined in on the fun. Shithead had created quite the stir.

The whole scene had the full attention of all the party-goers next door, but they pretty much kept doing what they were doing. They weren't the kind of folks that were going to let a little thing like a police raid ruin a good barbeque. The police had already gained entry to the home by the time I got out of my car. They were only in there a few minutes before one of the officers in charge came out onto the front porch and waved for me to walk up to where he was. I asked another officer to keep an eye on Shithead and went up to see what was happening.

It turned out that a little old lady lived in the house alone. She was shocked and dumbfounded when the police arrived. One of the officers actually knew her pretty well and assured the others that she was a law-abiding citizen. It was quickly determined that the fugitive wasn't there and she had never even heard of him. This all meant that Shithead had pointed out the wrong house. The only question now was to find out why. Was his entire story a lie? Had he just chickened out at the last minute and pointed out a random house? The officers wanted answers, so they headed towards my car.

They opened both of my back doors and started questioning Shithead from two sides. They knew that he had been lying and they were determined to find out why. But they weren't going to get anywhere with him. He buried himself into the floorboard, covered his head, shut down, and started begging us all to please take him to jail. He was terrified that someone on the block might see him, and it was clear that he was done talking. The officers were pissed and so was I. But one of them was a little madder than the rest of us and he was going to make him pay for this huge waste of time and resources. He dragged Shithead out of the car in front of God, the neighbors, and everybody. His jig was up, and it was only going to get worse.

A couple of officers led him out into the middle of the street, parading him right in front of the party next door. Several other neighbors had gathered by now, along with several cars that had stopped to see the show. Tears were rolling down Shithead's face at this point. Pulling him out of the car was a genius move, in my opinion. Not only had his entire world just collapsed in around him, but his drug dealing days in this area were over. People immediately started yelling out and calling him a rat. Shithead's tear ducts had achieved maximum output. His tough guy image couldn't have been any further in the rear-view mirror. Just about the time that I was wondering how things could have possibly gotten worse for this guy, I found out.

One of the officers raised his voice over the crowd and asked for everyone's attention. When everyone had quieted down, he announced to all the bystanders that we had been on the block today looking for a fugitive on a tip from Shithead. He used the fugitive's actual name and also told everyone Shithead's full name. He said that he appreciated good citizens like Shithead who were so eager to work with the police, patted him on the head, and thanked everyone for their attention. Then, he simply handed Shithead back over to me and said that we were done here. In less than a minute, we were all gone and the neighborhood was back to normal. As normal as it could have been, anyway.

The ride to jail was relatively uneventful, other than the obvious. Shithead cried the entire way, saying over and over that he was a dead man. I tried to assure him that people had short memories, and reminded him that he would be safe in jail for at least a few weeks. None of that seemed to be of any consolation to him. I also tried my best to drag the truth out of him but he never gave it up. I truly believed that he knew where the fugitive had been hiding and just backed out of the deal the last minute. Overall, though, I found it amusing that just an hour ago he was dreading going to jail, and now he was terrified of getting out. There was a hilarious kind of dirtbag irony to that. After all, he had made his own bed and now he was going to have to sleep in it. For how long was another question.

I never saw Shithead again. He went from a neighborhood staple to a ghost in the blink of an eye. A few years later, I arrested a girl from his block and I asked her about him on the way to jail. "Oh, that snitch moved somewhere to Ohio a few years ago," she told me. "Niggas was looking to kill his bitch ass." Not long after that, the fugitive that everyone had been searching for was located and arrested. He had been picked up somewhere outside of Houston, TX. You will have to decide for yourself if Shithead ever knew anything or not.

There's nothing quite like arresting your fugitive and getting a great deal on an air compressor at the same time.

CRIMINAL CASE STORIES

Not every story in this line of work centers on a big chase and an arrest. There are plenty of crazy tales to be found inside some of the criminal charges themselves. The ridiculous situations that these dipshits have gotten themselves into over the years could provide us all with a lifetime of laughs and entertainment. When you have worked in this industry for as long as I have, you will learn the true meaning of the phrase, "stranger than fiction." I thought I would share a few of those shorter stories with you here.

* * *

DON'T ROLL YOUR EYES AT ME - I once had a blind client that was arrested and charged with driving under the influence of alcohol. And even though he had been blind since he was a teen and had never possessed a driver's license, he was technically guilty as far as the law was concerned. If you find yourself scratching your head on this one, I understand why. Let me explain to you how that's even possible.

He had been out drinking with three of his friends one night when their car ended up in a muddy ditch. All four of them were drunk, and that wouldn't be the last stupid thing they would do that night. After trying unsuccessfully to get the car free under its own power, they decided to try pushing it out. A couple of them were rocking the car back and forth, while a third drunk was behind the wheel. They couldn't quite get the car free, so they came up with a new idea. Three of them needed to be pushing instead of two.

So, in their intoxicated wisdom, they put the blind guy behind the wheel and instructed him how to press the accelerator and brake accordingly as they rocked the car back and forth. What could possibly go wrong? They implemented their genius plan and had the car rocking pretty good when they heard the police sirens coming. So, they did what any drunks might do when they see the police coming. They jumped the guard rail and ran off into the woods. This left their sightless buddy there to fend for himself. Imagine the scene when the police arrived. Tires were spinning, mud was flying, and a drunken blind man was behind the wheel.

I felt like this entire charge and criminal case was a waste of time. It should have never been set for a court date, but it was. Just before going into the courtroom, they offered the defendant a plea deal. They agreed to drop the DUI charge if he would plead guilty to reckless driving. This would also result in him losing his driver's license for six months. I really wish that I could tell you that he rolled his eyes when they offered him that deal, but it was impossible to know behind those dark glasses. Either way, he took the deal and moved on with his life. I haven't kept up with him, but I feel like his driving record has probably been spotless since that night.

* * *

HAPPY BIRTHDAY - I once bonded a guy out of jail on the morning after his birthday for driving under the influence the night before. That fact alone didn't really stand out as remarkable until I looked at his file. One glance at his history told me that I had bonded him out the year before, also for DUI, and also on the day after his birthday. I tried to have a little fun with him, but he wasn't able to see in humor in it at all. This charge meant loss of his license for one year, so I told him that if he hurried, maybe he could get his driving privileges back just in time for next year's party. He was still not amused. I did manage to suggest that maybe, next year, he should celebrate at home.

***

MARRIED MORONS / TOGETHER FOREVER - I once had two ex-clients that married each other. Both of them had run from me on separate occasions and were on my shitlist. (Every bondsman has a shitlist full of people to never deal with again.) In both cases, the families had grown extremely angry about the wanted posters that I had placed on social media. There were hundreds of nasty comments on each wanted poster, along with several arguments from people on both sides of the law. Because of all the publicity, it hadn't taken me long to locate, arrest, and jail either one of them. So, it was interesting news on social media when the two of them got married. Their families both hated me, making threatening social media posts and even calling my office. But it all calmed down eventually. For a while, anyway.

After getting married, these two idiots went on a drug-fueled crime spree that made the local newspapers. The hunt for them by law enforcement got heated and kept our local social media buzzing. They were arrested within a few days of each other and placed into jail, remaining there through Valentine's Day. I seized this opportunity to make a new Facebook post. Sure, I really had no dog in this latest fight, but we had a history and they deserved whatever they got.

The wife had a picture of a custom license plate on her social media. It was one of those cheesy plates that you might get made at the beach or at the county fair. It had two hearts on it with their names inside, and it also said "Together Forever." I made a collage with a pic of that plate along with their two mugshots and incarceration dates. I posted it on Facebook with a smart-ass comment about them being so in love with each other that they even spent Valentine's Day together in jail. That post sent their families over the edge. But it was good for several days-worth of entertainment, fun, and threats. That post still gets shared every now and then. To this day, these two continue to land in and out of jail regularly and I rarely pass an opportunity to let social media know about it.

* * *

MORE MARRIED MORONS / THINKING INSIDE THE BOX - I have another wannabe Bonnie and Clyde story for you. These two specialized in shoplifting to fuel their drug addictions. Clyde would do the bulk of the stealing and then Bonnie would return the merchandise. Most stores only give out store credit gift cards for this type of caper, so they would sell the cards for cash. This lovely couple quickly graduated from small items to the big time. Before long, they were stealing chain saws, snow blowers, and other high dollar items. They were in and out of jail regularly for these shady shenanigans, until they each found a way to land themselves a real sentence.

They were driving along in their car one day, doing whatever it is that shitheads do, when they saw someone that they knew walking down the road. She was another local drug addict, known to everyone in my world. They decided to stop and give the girl a ride, not knowing that ride would end up being 10-15 years long. Their passenger saw a bottle of pills in the car and decided that she was going to steal it. She waited until the car was stopped, grabbed the bottle, jumped out of the car, and ran.

Clyde stopped the car, and he and Bonnie chased the girl into the woods. From what I understand, it was quite the chase. The girl ended up hiding from them for a little while, but they eventually caught her. Bonnie held her down while Clyde searched her for the missing pill bottle. It was nowhere to be found. She didn't want to tell them where she had hidden it, so the two decided to try to get the information out of her the old-fashioned way. They started to beat it out of her. Say what you will about a good beating, but it's a tried and true method.

Bonnie held her down by her hair while she and Clyde both roughed her up. They beat her almost unconscious before she finally told them where they could find their pill bottle. They wouldn't have to go far to retrieve it. She had hidden it inside her vagina. See, that's when most normal people would have just written that bottle of pills off as a total loss. I mean, just chalk it right up to the cost of doing business, as far as I'm concerned. But something as trivial as a little meth head muff wasn't going to keep these two from getting high. They went in after it.

There's no need to go into detail about the procedure that followed. It was pretty basic, really, and you can probably figure it out on your own. Anyway, Bonnie just kept on holding her down and Clyde went in for the snatch, pardon the pun. A few minutes later, they were in possession of what they came for. They simply left old girl in the woods and went on about their day.

It wasn't long before they were arrested for kidnapping, malicious wounding, and rape. By the letter of the law, they were guilty of all three charges. Their defense was that she was hiding their stolen property inside of her and had refused to return it on her own. They also argued that there was no sexual element to the crime at all. It's true that you never know what a jury might do, but no one was going to buy that bullshit. Both were still in prison the last time I checked.

* * *

HOLD MY CALLS PLEASE – Sadly, there is no shortage of vagina stories in this business, but I'm only sharing one more. I once got a phone call from the state police about a girl that I had placed into jail just a few hours earlier. They wanted to know all of the details of the arrest. Where did I find her? What was she doing? Was she dressed? What was she wearing? Did we stop anywhere on the way to jail? I was happy to answer all of their questions, but certainly curious as to why they were asking. The arrest had gone down quite easily. She was dressed in jeans and a tee shirt when I found her at her residence. She hadn't run from me or even tried to hide. I also let them know that I had high-definition cameras in my truck, which would show the entire ride to the jail if they wanted to view it. Curiosity was killing me and I had to ask, "Why are you asking me all this?"

"Because her vagina is ringing," he told me. I had to ask him to repeat that. "Her vagina is ringing," he said again. The jail had called the police because the defendant had a cell phone inside of her. They knew that because it had been ringing, and she had refused to take it out and surrender it. The police were in the process of obtaining some sort of warrant that would allow them to take her to a hospital and have it removed. They just wanted to know if I may have known when she put it there. I assured them that it was news to me. My guess is that she did it when I first knocked on her door. She had probably saw me, knew that she was going to jail, and did it in a rush. You would think that she would have at least taken the time to put it on silent. Or maybe vibrate?

* * *

CORPUS ABDUCTUS - I once had a client who stole a hearse. She and her girlfriend were in trouble regularly, so I was familiar with her before this even happened. It was a cold winter night and she was out walking around drunk. She found the hearse running in front of a funeral home and it must have looked like a warm refuge from the weather. The charges may not have made such a local buzz if it hadn't been for the body in the back of the car. But the caper really didn't get full traction until a locally published tabloid ran the story in print and on their social media page. Before we go any further, it's important to note that the jail she was placed in is located in a town called Beaver. The headline read, "Lesbian Snatches Stiff and Ends Up in Beaver." I couldn't have written it any better myself.

* * *

THERE'S NO SCHOOL ON SUNDAYS - What's crazier than stealing a hearse? Several 911 calls started rolling in late one night about a school bus running cars off of the road. It was nearly midnight on a Sunday, so the red flags were flying early on this one. This quickly resulted in a police pursuit that literally took a strange turn. The driver turned off of the pavement and headed up a steep, muddy road that wound up a mountain. Somehow, the school bus got further up that mountain than the police could, and they had to call the fire department for an off-road vehicle.

And it's a good thing the fire department responded. When they located the bus, the defendant was asleep in one of the passenger seats. If that wasn't strange enough, the bus was still running, in gear, and the back wheels were spinning in the mud. The rear tires actually caught on fire before they could get the engine stopped.

It turned out that I knew the defendant very well. He was a local drunk who had previously been into some petty criminal mischief, but nothing like this. I kept up with the case as it progressed and I'm glad that I did. It was revealed at the trial that the defendant had recently been prescribed lithium. The doctor that gave it to him must not have been aware that he was a known alcoholic, because lithium and alcohol can have serious side effects. In this case, the side effect was driving a school bus into the mountains until it caught on fire. I bet they didn't mention that on the TV commercial.

Before it was over, the prosecution was forced to drop the grand theft auto charge. As in most states, they would have had to prove that the defendant "intended to permanently deprive the owner of the vehicle" to make that charge stick. No one was going to believe that the old boy had planned to paint flowers on the bus and start following the Grateful Dead, so he ended up pleading to joyriding.

* * *

BROTHERLY LOVE - I once had a client who was charged with killing his brother. The defendant was at home and on supervised probation when the incident happened. He wasn't allowed to have alcohol in his home when the victim stopped by with a case of beer, already drunk. This was a violation of the defendant's probation and he didn't want any part of it. Asking his brother to leave several times soon turned into an actual fight. The fight led to the defendant stabbing his brother. After being stabbed, the brother took his case of beer, left the house, and went walking down the driveway. He probably felt like he had overstayed his welcome by that point. The defendant went to bed and fell asleep.

Early the next morning, a school bus driver discovered a dead body beside the road. This quickly led the police to the victim's brother's house, just up the road. When questioned, the defendant casually confessed to the entire thing. When the police asked him why he didn't call 911 after the stabbing, he had a very interesting answer. "I just thought he would walk home and be fine, as usual," he said. "I didn't call 911 the last two times I stabbed him either."

* * *

THAT'S NO TURKEY! - Oddly enough, I have encountered two cases of one brother stabbing and killing another. This next one happened on Thanksgiving, at the dinner table. Two brothers were fighting over which one was going to do the honors, when the argument escalated into a wrestling match over the carving knife. The only thing that ended up getting carved up that day was one of the brothers. The thing that makes this story stand out was the old west mentality and simple attitude of the family. They actually rallied against the prosecution in an effort to get the defendant released. In their view, this was a family issue, and it should have been left for the family to resolve. "It wasn't like he killed a stranger," his mom said. "He was one of our own." These people do still exist out there.

* * *

RACIST GRAMMAR - I had a client that was charged with a hate crime several years ago. When it happened, the entire "hate crime" issue was relatively new, so it was big news in such a small community. The victims were a black family that moved into a very rural and secluded community. Most of the residents there had grown up poor and had little education. Someone had burnt a cross in their front yard and spray painted a message on their mobile home within just a few days of their arrival. I'm not sure how the defendant had been linked to the crime, but he ended up confessing to everything, almost as if he were proud of himself.

One of the deputies laughed at him and told him that he hadn't even spelled the message on the home correctly, and that pissed him off. "I did spell it right," he insisted. The deputy quickly gave him a marker and a piece of paper. "Here, write down exactly what you wrote on the trailer," he told him. The defendant grabbed the marker, and did just as he was instructed. He proudly slid the paper back to the deputy and said, "See, I know how to fucking spell." That piece of paper was entered into evidence, because it was the exact phrase that was painted on the trailer, and spelled exactly the same way. "Niger go home."

* * *

ROUND TWO! - I once had a defendant that was arrested for fighting with two deputies. The officers had responded to a call of a person laying in the middle of the road and found him unresponsive when they arrived. After shaking him awake, the defendant jumped up and started punching them. They eventually got him subdued and arrested him. The defendant was a well-known shithead in the area, but had never been known to fight with the police, so I asked him what had happened. His story almost made me feel bad for him.

He had been walking home that night when a car pulled up to him. He was blinded by the headlights when two guys got out of the car and jumped him. One was holding him while the other one had presumably beat him unconscious. When the police arrived and woke him up, the defendant had not experienced any lapse of time, so he thought he was still in the midst of the original fight. To him, it was nothing short of mass confusion. One second, he was fighting two local thugs over an unpaid debt, and the next second, he said that they suddenly turned into police officers. The shit these people get themselves into is more interesting than any fiction out there.

☎ ☎ ☎

ME: This is the second domestic battery your son has been charged with this month. It sounds like he needs to stay away from that woman.

HER: Oh no, that woman is still in the hospital. This charge is with his new girlfriend.

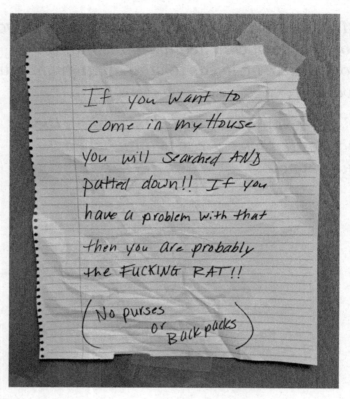

   This note pretty much admits that there is illegal activity going on inside, and would very likely qualify as enough "probable cause" to obtain a search warrant.

NOBODY HAS A KNIFE LIKE THAT

Privately funded fugitive recovery is a subject that I haven't mentioned in either book yet, so let's talk about it now. This happens when a private citizen uses their property to post someone's bond, and then wants to revoke it at a later date. Sometimes, this occurs because the property owner wants to sell or use the property for collateral on a loan. Neither is possible while a piece of property is being held for a bond. Sometimes it happens simply because the defendant is being difficult to deal with or on drugs so bad that the family feels like he would be safer in jail. Whatever the reason may be, the property owner can't just go out and arrest the defendant and take him to jail. They have to hire a licensed agent to do it for them.

I have done many of these over the years and find them much easier to do than regular arrests. This is mainly due to the fact that the property owner will do most of the leg work for you. They can generally tell you exactly when and where the defendant will be, eliminating the entire searching phase. Most of the time, it's someone who lives in the same house with them, making it simple enough to be let into the home while the defendant is sound asleep. But it's not always that simple.

It was early on a freezing winter morning and pouring the snow when we took this particular private job. The defendant was a young boy from a very good family who was worried about him. They felt like jail was the best place for him at the time and I could not have agreed more. He was staying at a drug house that was very well known to everyone in the world of law enforcement. The place was owned by an ex-convict and had been the scene of more than one overdose. I offered another agent, Pedro, half the bounty and we headed up there. Pedro was exactly the kind of guy you wanted with you if you were going in to one of these shit holes. He was a black belt in jiu jitsu and taught the same in his own gym. He also enjoyed traveling around to kick people's asses in other states in his free time. That being said, he was still mild mannered, good with people, and didn't lose his temper until he needed to. With my temperament as shitty as it is, Pedro was usually the voice of reason when we were out in the field.

I knew this place well. I grew up about a mile away from it and could remember back when it was a decent home. I used to ride my bicycle by it daily and it was sad to see the state this neighborhood was in now. It was situated right on the main road with no way to sneak in. There were also several cameras on the property, so there was nothing to do but pull right in, knock on the door, and hope for the best. So that's exactly what we did.

You could tell from the snow that no one had used the front door in some time. All the foot traffic had been using the rear entrance that was covered by a small porch. Pedro knocked on the door even as two extremely outdated cameras were looking us right in the face. I'm not sure if they worked or not, but we had to assume they already knew we were here. I figured that our chances of ever getting inside were slim to none. But we got lucky.

A teenage boy came to the door, opened it, and walked out onto the porch with us. Pedro asked him if our defendant was inside the house. The boy was clearly mentally challenged with a severe speech impediment, but he told us that our guy was inside sleeping. He also told us that he wasn't allowed to let anyone inside without his dad's permission, but he wasn't home right now. He struggled through the entire conversation. We promised him that were only there to arrest the defendant and that we weren't interested in anyone else. This is where I would have usually threatened to arrest him for harboring a fugitive, but he seemed fragile and I didn't want to scare him unless I had to.

  I suggested that he call his dad and put him on the phone with me. He took his phone out, put it on speaker, and called his dad. He even stuttered when he was dialing. I didn't think he would ever get the number punched in. I was calculating just what I was going to say to his dad, even knowing that there was no way in hell he was going to let us in. But he never answered. The boy tried a few times while we talked, but good ol' dad never picked up. Pedro told the boy that the police were on the way and they were going to kick the door in when they got there. That scared this kid to death. Pedro said that this could all be avoided by just letting us inside. "Your dad is gonna be pissed when this door gets torn off in this weather," Pedro told him. "He's really gonna be mad when he finds out that you could have stopped it." He immediately let us in because Pedro might have just scared the stutter out of him. Some folks would have felt bad for this kid, but not me. I wanted my guy and I would have probably kicked that door in to get him before long anyway.

The kid took us straight to our boy. He was sleeping on the floor with a young girl. There were also several other people sleeping on air mattresses that were scattered about here and there. We scared the shit out of our guy when we woke him up, but we were trying to keep the whole ordeal quiet. The less people that we woke up, the better off we would all be. He was clearly not going to be any trouble. You could tell at first glance that he wasn't the type of kid that was going to fight with the two of us. He was very confused, however, as to why he was being arrested. We told him to get dressed as quick as he could and we would explain it all to him in the vehicle. We needed to get the hell out of this joint. He had just got his jeans on when the whole operation took a turn.

Some dude came down the hall with a knife, yelling for us to get the fuck out of his house. When I say knife, I don't mean a pocket knife. This dude was toting a big ass, shiny, fuck off, Crocodile Dundee knife. The kind of ridiculous knife you might see on display at a flea market in

Kentucky with a built-in compass. Nobody actually buys them. I had no idea who this fucker was, but he was pissed and waking up everybody in the damn place. I threw our kid at Pedro, drew my Glock, and pointed it straight at his chest. "Drop that knife, motherfucker, or I will kill you right now," I yelled at him. He stopped in his tracks, but only for a few seconds. "You can't kill me in my own house," he said. But he said it like a question, as if he was pondering the legalities of it.

I glanced at Pedro, who had also drawn down with one hand and was holding our guy with the other. Dude took a step forward and I screamed at him again. "Motherfucker, don't make me shoot you! Drop that goddamn knife!" I told him that we were leaving there with this boy and there was no reason for him to get killed in the process. That's when he tried to rally his troops against us. It was true that we were outnumbered, but this entire bunch was soft and barely awake. "You can't shoot us all, bitch," he said. "I will stab you before you can get to the door." He could not have been more wrong.

My .357 SIG was loaded with 15 rounds and I absolutely could have shot all of them if I needed to. My Glock was still trained on him when I yelled, "You are the first motherfucker getting shot, so you will never know, will you?" Now, one of his own people was telling him to drop the knife, but he never did. Pedro and I backed out the door, guns drawn, with dude moving towards us the entire time. It was slow going, with us both yelling back and forth the whole way out. He never rushed us and I knew that he wasn't going to at that point. I would have certainly killed him if he had and he knew that to be a fact. It was more of a mutual retreat and he kept the same distance between us. He got to look like a badass in front of his friends and we got out with our guy.

The snow was still flying and about a foot deep on the ground while we were dragging that poor kid to the vehicle. Remember, all he was wearing was a pair of jeans and a terrified look on his face. He had never seen anything like that before unless it was on TV. Pedro threw him across the back seat, jumped in with him, and we tore out of there before anyone could get dressed and chase after us.

I was driving down the road when Pedro said, "Did you see the size of that fucking knife?" I immediately started laughing and he wanted to know what the fuck was so funny. I was laughing about that damn knife. I couldn't help myself. It was absolutely ridiculous. I'm telling you, nobody actually has a knife like that. If you were filming a movie and wanted the biggest knife on earth for comedy effect, that one would have been too big. What were the chances of someone actually pulling one out in a confrontation? I told Pedro, "If we had spent two more minutes in that house, someone would have been dead." He disagreed with that. "Someone would have been dead in two more SECONDS," he said. Then we both laughed about it for a bit.

    The kid thought that we were insane. He had just been standing in the middle of a good old-fashioned Mexican standoff and we were laughing about it. I admit that it had been hectic, but we had seen worse. We apologized to the kid for dragging him through the snow like we did, but it wasn't like we had a choice. On the way to jail, we both preached to him quite a bit about the consequences of his recent actions. "What if I had killed that guy?" I asked him. "What if I had been killed? Or you?" We told him that his mother sent us there because she loved him, and that he needed to think about his decisions in the future. You never can tell if you get through to them.

I ran into his mother some years later. She told me that he had never been in trouble since that incident and that he was doing very well. She said that he had earned a degree and was now working a well-paid technical job. Even though that shithead with the knife probably had more to do with it than me and Pedro did, it's always good to hear things like that.

☎ ☎ ☎

ME: There's nothing worse than a lying drug dealer.

HIM: I'm not a liar and stop calling me a drug dealer!

ME: Dude, I just took over 200 pills and $2,300 out of your cargo pocket.

HIM: These ain't even my pants, man! Somebody else put that shit in there!

ME: Well, they were nice enough to put your wallet and ID in there, too.

CLEAN COAL TECH.
$100 BILLION to DEVELOP
PINN. INDIAN AND ELKhorn
CREEK Dry FEED By POND
AND Ditches. DRINKING
WATER, FISH CRAW
DADS AND MINNOWS
GONE. CHEMICALS
GLOWING

SPECULATORS
HOG By BIRTH
HOG By NATURE
AND
HOGS By ACTS
OF THE
LEGISLATURE

The big cities get their fancy graffiti and their beautifully painted train cars. We get this shit in the Appalachians. I really have no idea what this one was about. I'm feeling like it is supposed to be some sort of backwoods, anti-coal company poetry, but I'm not really sure. Feel free to email me with your interpretations.

IT STILL HURTS WHEN I PEE

This particular fugitive had skipped out on some sort of EPA charges. He had been caught dumping dangerous chemicals into a stream from a small shop he owned and they were coming at him hard. After looking for him for some time, I got a call one day from someone who told me where he had been hiding. This caller told me what he had been driving and even told me that he was there right at that moment. I knew that the caller was correct about the vehicle he had been driving, so I decided to treat the rest of the information seriously as well. I grabbed Bobby and we headed out.

The place was very easy to find and the defendant's truck was parked in the driveway. The caller had been right. It was an apartment above a very tall garage with a steep set of stairs leading up to it. There was only one way in and out, so we just walked up and knocked on the door. No response. We kept knocking and letting him know who we were, but still no response. There was a large house next door that was painted to match this building, so I decided to walk over and talk to the residents while Bobby watched the apartment. A nice, older woman came to the door and said that she did, in fact, own and rent that apartment. I showed her a picture of the fugitive and she immediately verified that he was her renter. She also told me that if his truck was there, he was there.

I told her that we had been knocking with no answer, and that we were probably going to have to kick the door in. She asked me not to do that and offered to give me the keys to the lock. That made everything much easier, so I thanked her and headed back. Bobby told me that he had heard movement behind the door, but still no voices. I once again announced very loudly who we were, that we now had a key, and that we were coming in with the owner's permission. I made it clear that we would need to see his hands and that we did not want to hurt him. Anyone inside would have certainly heard the warnings. Then, I unlocked the door.

He was definitely inside the apartment. The safety chain was latched, which could have only been done from the inside. He had also pushed an old school projector television up against the door, along with the couch and a few other things. This guy was barricaded in and this was going to be a pain in the ass. The owner was now standing down in the driveway, watching, and she wasn't going to like this at all. I asked her to please yell up to him and see if she could talk him into coming out. She tried that, but he still never responded. I knew that it probably wasn't going to work, but I wanted to try everything that I could before tearing that door down. But that's what I was about to do.

The owner immediately started throwing a fit. She was clearly very attached to that door. I had already made it clear that there were no other options and that she could take the door out of his deposit, but that was no help. The door was a real pain to breach. Doors are usually fairly easy to tear down, but that changes when someone has it barricaded. This always makes it much tougher and takes longer. Plus, during the process, you still have to be prepared for what's on the other side. You can't exactly just reach your arm in and unlock it, unless you wanted to lose an arm. You need to be careful, while also being prepared for a fight. Or, even worse, a gun. This particular door actually broke into two separate pieces after several kicks. The bottom half became completely detached and we threw it out of the way. The top half was then left hanging by only that safety chain, and easy enough to get around. Then, it was just a matter of pushing through a stack of furniture. It took a few minutes, but we got through. Dumbass was waiting on the other side.

He didn't have a weapon and he wasn't hiding. He was barely even dressed. He was stripped down to his whitey tighties, crouched into a fighting position, and charged me the second I was in his sight. That's when I realized that he was oiled up. You read that right. This crazy bastard had oiled himself up in an effort to keep us from getting ahold of him. What was his plan? Was he just going to try to slip past us and run off into the woods in his underwear? Whatever his end game was, I was having one hell of a time fighting with him. He was a bit bigger than me and covered in what I guessed was baby oil. I really didn't know what it was but it made this one of the weirdest wrestling matches that I had ever been part of. We both went to the floor within seconds. Bobby barely had room to get through the door, the room was small, and he couldn't be of too much immediate help. I was on this guy's back, trying to choke him with my left arm and punching him with my right. I must have looked like a kid trying to catch a greased pig at the county fair. I was yelling at Bobby to keep the exit blocked, because if this pig had gotten out that door, he might still be out running and glistening in the wild today.

I was begging him to stop fighting and telling him that I didn't want to hurt him. He wasn't listening or letting up, so I started making my punches count. I started landing hard ones to his right kidney, one after the next. Several didn't seem to have an effect, but I knew exactly which one did the damage. I actually felt the wind go out of him on impact. It sounded like his lungs deflated for just a second, his arms failed him, and he collapsed to the ground. We got handcuffs and leg chains on him as fast as we could and while the fight was gone out of him. He acted like he was really hurt, but I didn't have time to care. And let's not forget that the property owner had now come up onto the porch and was yelling about her door. She kept repeating that she had given me a key in order to avoid all of this. I kept trying to tell her that he had locked the chain and that key could not have saved her door. She just didn't seem to get it.

We ended up letting him put pants and a shirt on before leaving. As we were heading down the steps, the property owner was still screaming about that goddamn door. I gave her a card, told her to call my office later, and headed towards the jail with Dumbass. He was still acting like he was badly hurt, but I had seen this act a hundred times before. I still didn't care either, because I was damn near as beat up as he was by this time. I was exhausted from tearing down the door, fighting this guy, and now I was covered in some sort of oil. And what the fuck was that all about, anyway? I never did get a straight answer out of him about that trick. We got him to the jail safely, and I thought I had seen the last of Dumbass. But that was not going to be the case at all.

A year or so later, another bonding company hired me to locate and arrest Dumbass for them. They had bonded him out after I last jailed him, and he was on the run again. This other company even provided me with a two-man team after I had got him located three counties away. We hopped into the vehicle early one morning and made the trip. I warned them on the way that he was a fighter and filled them in on my last run-in with him. We weren't going to have a replay of that today, however, because we were going to his new place of employment.

We got there just before daylight, and spoke to a security guard. He knew Dumbass very well. He wasn't due in for another hour or so, and the security guard took us to where he would be parking. He also told us what he would be driving, so this was going to be a piece of cake. One of the guys sat in the vehicle and would be blocking Dumbass in when he parked. The other two of us were going to extricate him from his car. It went just as planned.

He pulled into a parking space and was instantly blocked in. Before he even knew what was happening, I had a sawed off .12 gauge pointed at his head, and one of the other guys had a pistol on the other side of him. He looked like a deer in headlights. He was living and working far enough away that he thought he was safe, but he had just learned better. We got him out and cuffed without incident. Oh, he talked shit and wanted to fight, but he knew better. Now, it was time for the long ride to jail.

Dumbass wouldn't quit running his mouth in the vehicle. All the way back, he kept begging to fight me. "Please take these cuffs off and I will beat your ass," he must have said at least twenty times. Of course, we couldn't do that, but I was curious to know why he wanted it so bad. He claimed that I had fucked up his kidneys the last time I arrested him. He gave us some sob story about bleeding from his ass for several days after our fight and said that ever since then, it hurt him to pee. I probably made things worse when I started laughing about that bullshit. I told him that there was no way a few kidney punches caused all that, and even if it had, fuck him anyway. I also reminded him that the last fight had been 100% his choice, not mine. I also told him that I had given him several chances to come out of that apartment peacefully. "Besides," I said, "we don't have time to stop at a drug store and buy you a bottle of baby oil." But he wasn't the kind of person that was ever going to understand real life, so he kept begging me to fight all the way to the jail. He even asked again while we were inside the jail, in front of the guards. I had to rub it in just a little, so I reminded him, "I damn near beat your kidneys out last time, so what makes you think you could win round two?" He was all talk and we knew it. We finally got him booked into jail custody, and this time, I really was going to be done with him forever.

After he had fled the same court case for a second time, his charges were picked up by the federal government. They were fed up with his antics and weren't going to give him another chance to run. This time around, he sat his ass in jail until trial. He was found guilty and was sentenced to fifteen years. He only did a few of those years before he died in prison. The newspaper article just said "from a long illness," but I'd like to think it was from complications from a kidney infection.

☹ ☹ ☹

HIM: They got me on a bullshit burglary charge again.

ME: Why is it bullshit?

HIM: You know that the cops only came to my house because I have a record.

ME: No, the cops came to your house because they followed the footprints in the snow from your neighbor's broken window.

It's funny enough to me that someone painted this on the side of a house, but I find it hilarious that someone took the time to respond to it. It's like a bad Facebook post for people without the internet.

LONG-DISTANCE DOUBLE-CROSS

I once had a fugitive that we believed was staying in a known drug house. We weren't 100% sure that he was in there, but several people were telling us the same story. If it was true, this was the kind of place that we were never going to get into without a full-blown fight on our hands. It would have taken half a dozen agents to gain entry properly. The owner had cameras on the house, cameras on the only road in, and cameras in the woods. Our information was pretty solid, but it wasn't enough to obtain a warrant to get us inside. We were going to have to take our time and get creative on this one. The first thing I did was to post a cash reward for him on social media and it didn't take long for the right call to come in.

The girl who called us had grown up with the fugitive and knew him very well. She had also helped me with information before, which I had paid her for, so I had a good relationship with her. She said that they used to run around and get high together until she moved a few hours away, got a job, and went to rehab. She was doing very well now and working, but was happy to help us for the reward money. She said that they still spoke via social media and that she was sure that she could lure him out into public. She said it would be easy because he had a crush on her and was always trying to have sex with her. So, the two of us worked together and hatched a plan. We concocted what we thought was the perfect story and she started messaging him. She kept me in the loop the entire time.

She told him that she had recently left rehab and had moved back home. Now there is a lie that's easy to believe, because damn near everyone who goes to rehab leaves before completing the program. I had asked her to take her time with him, so they spoke a little back and forth for a few days before she finally asked him if they could get together. He quickly agreed, but this wasn't going to be exactly that simple. He told her that he couldn't have her come to where he was staying, and that he would have to walk to the end of the road where she could pick him up. He said that he stayed with people who didn't allow him to have any visitors, so they were going to have to find some place to go. Keep in mind that this girl is actually four hours away and running this entire conversation by me as it progresses. She said all the right things and it didn't take long to learn that he was exactly where we thought he was. Now, it was time to lure him out of there.

The meeting time and place was quickly set at the end of the road from where he was staying. He asked her what she would be driving, so I had her to describe my girlfriend's actual vehicle to him. Then, I had my girlfriend go park that car at the meeting place where it could easily be seen by someone who might be walking in that direction. Why would I put my girlfriend in a position like that? Simple. Because he was never even going to get anywhere near that car. I was already in the area with two other agents and ready for action.

The three of us hid my truck out of sight and set up an ambush in the woods about 200 yards before the end of the road. We were set up in such a way that we would triangulate him and give him nowhere to go. It wasn't long before we saw him coming. He could see my girlfriend's car at the end of the road, so that's probably why he wasn't even attempting to be cautious. He was just walking along casually, listening to his headphones, without a care in the world. Until he got to us, anyway.

We scared the hell out of him when we jumped out of the woods. He never saw us coming. And with those headphones on, he never heard us either. He was just jamming to some tunes one second, and then bam! Things had just gone from "date casual" to "serious business" in about one second for this poor bastard. My two buddies were just poised for a fight or a chase, but I had my sawed-off shotgun right on him. With the music in his ears, I guess he couldn't hear me yelling for him to get on the ground. I yelled and motioned with the shotgun for him to get down, but he never did. I couldn't tell if he was planning to run for it, or maybe he was just in shock. Either way, I wasn't going to have to tell him again. One of my guys planted him in the ditch and tore the headphones off of his head. He was handcuffed before he even knew who we were. He thought we were the police at first, but we cleared that up pretty quickly after he came back to his senses.

On the walk back to my truck, I texted our informant an update. You all know that most of the people we arrest aren't Nobel Peace Prize winners, but this guy was extra dumb. He actually had no clue how we had found him and it never entered his mind that this had all been a set up. He even asked us if we could please let his friend at the end of the road know that he was under arrest, so that she wouldn't sit there waiting on him. I mean, did he think that we just happened to be hiding in the woods when he was walking up that road? What an idiot.

We never want to give away an informant's identity, but sometimes it's very difficult to keep them anonymous. I thought that this would be one of those times, but it turned out that it was actually going to be pretty easy. I just used the name of the drug dealer he was staying with, and told him that's who had ratted him out. "He said that he was sick of you and promised to call us the next time you planned to leave," I told him. Dude didn't doubt it for even a second. He started ranting and swearing that he was going to kill him when he got out of jail. I even let him message his friend, who he thought was parked up the road, to tell her that he was under arrest. At the same time, I called my girlfriend and told her to drive away before we got any closer. It had all worked out even more perfectly than planned.

On the way to jail, and to further protect my informant, I made matters even worse for him. I made up all sorts of bad shit that the local drug dealer had said about him. "He said you were a big pussy and he even refused to take the reward money that I offered him," I told him. "He said he didn't want the damn money, he just wanted rid of you." Dude was more pissed than ever and it was awesome. Look at it this way. We had our fugitive and protected our informant's identity. She was going to get her money, and with any luck, this one would kill a drug dealer when he got out of jail. It was truly a win for everyone.

This Facebook post got really popular, really quickly. The defendant started calling right way, demanding that I take it down. She refused to turn herself in, so it stayed up until we eventually found her. Someone said that the big knot on her head looked like a "methsquito bite." This is exactly why I hate touching these nasty addicts.

SHORT STORIES

Not all chase and arrest stories are quite insane enough to warrant their own chapters. For the most part, believe it or not, interactions can go relatively smoothly. But things tend to move quickly when emotions are high, so it isn't out of the ordinary for a calm arrest to take a strange or unexpected turn. I thought that I would share some of those shorter, but memorable, elements with you here.

* * *

CHOKED BY A CORPSE - Bobby and I were transporting a female prisoner to North Carolina late one evening. We were hired by a bonding company down there to locate and arrest her after they found out that she was hiding from them in our area. She was a known drug addict, easy to find, and we arrested her without incident. It was a different story after we hit the road. She hadn't fought with us at all up to that point, but she got a little antsy when we didn't get off of the highway at the local jail exit. When we explained to her that we were going to turn her over to her bondsman from Charlotte, she became very upset. I'm not sure what the difference had been to her, but she certainly didn't want to go back to NC. I told her to shut the fuck up and gave her the typical speech about how it would be easier on us all for her to just relax and deal with it. She seemed to calm down and I continued driving south.

But what we had mistaken for calm was really just her plotting against us. Somehow, without us realizing it, she had gotten her handcuffs in front of her. I had seen this done a dozen times, and it's really quite the feat, but I had never seen it accomplished that quietly. She waited to make her move in a tunnel as were entering into Virginia. I never saw it coming. As soon as we hit the tunnel, she threw her arms around my neck. Pulled back, and was choking me with the handcuff chain. I don't know if you have ever been choked with handcuffs in a tunnel at 70 mph, but it's rather off-putting.

I don't know what she was trying to accomplish. Kill me? Kill herself? Kill us all? Escape? Catch new charges? Any and all of those options would have just made her situation worse. Bobby earned his money that night. He instantly began to pull her off of me. The only hold he could get on her was her neck, so now, two out of three of us can't breathe. Don't forget that I am trying to stop a speeding vehicle without crashing. I barely accomplished that mission, and immediately peeled her off of me. Bobby was now actually in the back seat with her, so I got the vehicle out of the tunnel and off of the road. I got out and jerked her door open with murder in my eyes. I drug that bitch out of the truck, planted her in the gravel, and placed the cuffs behind her back, where they belong. It was not a kind or gentle process. I didn't care that all the traffic that we had just stopped was now creeping by for an eyeful. I guess it isn't every day that you see someone fighting in a tunnel. When I secured her back into the truck, I grabbed her by the chin with one hand and the back of the head with the other. I had intended to give her a bad case of "shaken crackhead syndrome," and scare her into submission.

But, when I grabbed her face, there was almost nothing to get a grip on. Instead of grasping her lower jaw as I had intended, my fingers damn near came together. It turned out that she had no bottom teeth and her lower jaw had deteriorated. It was like grabbing a rotten, dusty corpse. But it was still enough to shake the shit out of her brain long enough for me to threaten to bury her somewhere in the woods. She was afraid for her life and you could see it in her eyes.

The rest of the trip was unremarkable and the crypt keeper made no more attempts on my life.

* * *

THAT TRUCK ISN'T GOING TO PASS INSPECTION - At least we had gotten through that last incident with no vehicle damage. One of our other agents, Pedro, wasn't always as lucky. He was once hauling a skinny little crackhead to jail who tried to get away from him while he was driving. She somehow got herself situated between his bucket seats and facing the rear of the vehicle. When Pedro slammed on the brakes, her skinny, crackhead, ass bone went straight through his windshield. She took his rear-view mirror with her when she went. No brand of windshield wiper cleaner was going to wipe that one off.

* * *

WHAT'S THAT SMELL? – A new windshield and mirror was going to be the least of Pedro's problems. A local, female police officer once helped him arrest a fugitive who had locked herself into a bathroom stall. This all went down at a local convenience store and they eventually got her into Pedro's vehicle. She was also a known crackhead, and you always have to expect the unexpected with them, but this one was going to go above and beyond. As long as she had been locked in that bathroom, I guess that she failed to use it, because she decided to take a shit in Pedro's truck. It wasn't an accident either, she was kind enough to tell him beforehand that she was going to do it. Now, Pedro's new rear-view mirror was going to need a couple of those Christmas tree air fresheners hung on it.

* * *

I DON'T KNOW WHERE HE IS, BUT I KNOW WHERE HE'S GOING TO BE - Pedro and I were once out in the middle of nowhere looking for a fugitive together. We had made a few trips out to this area but were having no luck. Everywhere we went it seemed that we were just a few hours behind him. We were just about to post a reward on social media when we received a call from a local resident. She heard that we were looking for this guy and wanted to know if there was a reward for him. I told her that there was not currently, but I was prepared to do something for her if she had any information that we could use. "I can lead you right to him early tomorrow morning," she said. When I asked her for more details, she simply said, "He will be in my bed and I will leave the door unlocked for you."

If this was true, I was prepared to give her a few hundred bucks for her trouble. But she made it much easier than that. "If you will buy me a Coke and a pack of cigarettes today, I promise you that he will be there in the morning," she told me. This might have been the craziest proposition I had ever heard and it sounded like fun, so this was an investment that I was prepared to make. We certainly weren't making any headway otherwise, so why not? We had to wait about an hour on this girl to meet us at the local store. When she arrived, we learned that she actually walked there. Unbelievable.

We bought her double what she had asked for. She scored two packs of smokes and two Cokes that day. She even got a free ride home from us. She told us to come back at 8 a.m. the following morning if we wanted to arrest our guy. She promised us that the door would be unlocked, and that the two of them would be in the bed asleep. As you can imagine, she was a very simple person. People like that are difficult to read, so Pedro and I had no idea what to expect the following morning. It was, however, the only lead that we had and we were going for it. We rolled in as scheduled, found the door unlocked, and found him asleep in the bed. We arrested him with no trouble while our girl was sitting on the couch enjoying a cigarette.

* * *

IT'S NIPPLY OUT HERE TONIGHT - I went into a house to arrest a girl one cold, rainy evening and found her watching television on the couch. She was wrapped up under a blanket and refused to get up when I asked her to. There was a police officer with me and we both tried to talk her into getting up on her own, but she still refused. I gave her more chances than I should have before I snatched the blanket off her and jerked her off of the couch. I was surprised to find her completely naked and ready to fight. The two of us had cuffs on her in just a few seconds, but she still refused to dress herself. This kind of bullshit is just a last resort grasp at trying to avoid arrest, and it always pisses me off. I simply drug her outside in the rain, and headed towards my truck with her. I let her stand outside in the cold for some time while I promised her that we were going to jail, naked or clothed. Traffic was driving by and I told her that she was going to be famous on social media within the hour. It didn't take her long to reverse her thinking and start begging me to take her back inside for clothes. I was already angry, so I met her half way. I let her put on some shorts, a tee shirt, and flip flops before chucking her back into the truck. I drove the hour or so to jail rolling her window down every time she tried to talk to me.

* * *

FUCK YOUR SHOES - I have seen all sorts of booby traps over the years. Trip wires, glass, nails, pits, and more. I have always been lucky enough to avoid them, except one. Bobby and I once parked several hundred yards away from a mobile home and walked in quietly. Some dude was standing in the living room and we just strolled right in on him. He told us that our female fugitive was asleep in the back bedroom. I headed down the hall just as the guy screamed, "Run, Baby! It's the law!" I wasn't worried about her getting away because I was almost to the room by that time. But I wasn't going to make it to the room. I fell through the floor all the way to my chest just as my fugitive came running out of the bedroom.

She nearly ran right over top of me and there was little that I could do about it. They had cut a huge hole into the floor and thrown a rug over it, so I was wrapped up and damn near helpless. Bobby was right behind me in the hall, so she was still unable to get anywhere. I wanted to kick somebody's ass by the time I got out of that redneck trap, but I didn't. She wasn't helping my temper by laughing right in my face about it. I was the one laughing as I drug her all the way back to the car at a jog, barefooted and begging for shoes.

* * *

SUCK ON THIS - I had a client charged with murder under the strangest of circumstances. Try and follow closely. He had been in a terrible fight with his wife and went out on a two-day drinking binge. He actually stayed in the woods drinking all night. At the end of day two, he went looking for her at a local bar. He walked up to a truck that two of his neighbors were sitting in and asked them, "Have you seen my wife?"

Let's backtrack a bit. His neighbors probably didn't know that he was about as drunk as a human could possibly be. They also couldn't have known that he had actually shot himself earlier that day, and was currently bleeding out. They could not have seen that he had that same gun in his jacket and had came there to kill his wife with it. Had they known any of those things, one of them would have almost certainly not have answered like he did.

"She's right here in the truck, giving us blowjobs," one of them said. Dude shot both of them and headed off towards the bar. Lucky for his wife and probably several other people, he collapsed before he got there, and was damn near dead when law enforcement responded.

* * *

DON'T BE SUCH A PUSSY - I went on a raid with an entire team of deputies one evening. They were looking for someone with a warrant at the same home that I believed a fugitive was hiding in. It was a known drug hang out and there could have been any number of people in there at any given time, so nearly a dozen officers showed up. They went in first and cleared the house before I came in. When I walked into the living room, they had seven or eight people lying on the floor. Everyone was in a neat row, with their hands behind their heads, as instructed. All of them were quiet except one. Of course, you know it was my fugitive. He was crying his eyes out like a little girl. Just as I walked over to take him into custody, he looked at the guy lying beside him and cried, "What in the world is going on?" The dude beside him was totally unshaken from the raid, and he answered my guy in a very matter of fact tone. "It's a fucking bust, dumbass. What does it look like?"

Local copper theft is such a serious problem in this area that it's caused major local power outages and several electrocution deaths. Copper thieves around here can strip your home of all its wire faster than you can go out and get a haircut. They even scaled a tower once on the roof of a local hospital. They stole the Medevac helicopter antennae and knocked the power out at the hospital for a few days. Brand new homes have been stripped of their copper before the new owners can move in. Sadly, signs like this are commonplace to let thieves know that these spools have no value at the local scrapyards.

BITCH ON A STICK

Two agents from an out-of-state bonding company once hired me to help them find and arrest a girl. She had fled their state and was hiding in an area that I was very familiar with, so local law enforcement had recommended that they get me involved. That worked out well for them, because I actually located the girl with just a few phone calls. It turned out that she had spent several years in my area, she had a local criminal history, and I knew exactly what calls to make. The three of us headed to where I was told that she was staying with her boyfriend.

I knew the area well. It was an apartment above a small business that I had driven by thousands of times. There was even a parking lot next door, perfectly situated for us to use in order to sneak up on the apartment on foot. So that's just what we did. There was only one entrance to the residence, so we all three went to the door and I knocked. A man eventually answered and I asked him to come out and talk to us on the porch. He agreed to come out, but he was very nervous. He swore that the girl we were looking for did not live there with him. He admitted to knowing her, but that was about it. He did not want us to search his apartment, but I made up a lie that changed his mind. It was a lie that I had used 100 times before.

I told him that we were going to stand guard at the door, call for a warrant, and also have a canine officer to come out and search the place. None of these people want that. There was almost a 100% chance that there were drugs in there, and we all knew it. I swore to him that we weren't interested in anything except our fugitive and he eventually let us in. I would have bet you a week's pay that she was in there, judging from his demeanor alone. We searched that place from top to bottom and couldn't find her. There were female's clothes, shoes, and toiletries, but no fugitive. He had told us that he lived here alone, but that was clearly a lie. At this point, I felt like she might have been out, and maybe we had ruined our shot at arresting her. So, in an effort to salvage the situation, I hatched a plan. I treated him like I believed him and like we were buddies. I told him that we all had to leave the state tonight, but promised that I would give him $500 if he was able to find out where she was staying. I acted like we were in a big hurry to get on the road, and we left the apartment.

My plan was to simply watch the place. I wanted him to think that we were long gone and hopefully catch her returning home. After watching the place for an hour or so, it had got dark outside. After a while, one of the out-of-state agents I was with said that he thought he saw two shadows inside, moving behind a window. It was hard for me to tell, so I decided to sneak up to the front door and see if I could learn anything. When I got near the door, I clearly heard the voices of a male and a female talking. I couldn't make anything out, but it certainly sounded like she was in there to me. The thought of that actually vindicated me, because I had believed she was in there the first time around. I called the other two agents up, and we knocked again, really hard and loud this time. The idea was to surprise and scare them.

I know what you're thinking. You are wondering why we didn't kick the door in. I simply did not have enough information to do that. Yes, I thought I heard a female, but there was no way to know for sure. Even if I had, I couldn't have known that it was her. If I had kicked that door in and been wrong, I could have been sued and held liable for damages. Also, I didn't really know these two guys I was with. Truthfully, I may have kicked it down if I had been working with my regular guys.

There was about one minute of commotion before he came to the door. I figured that she was hiding again. I wasn't going to have a friendly conversation with him this time. The second that door opened, the three of us plowed past him and started searching again. He was raising hell the entire time, yelling for us to get out of his apartment, but that wasn't going to happen. He even threatened to call the police on us two or three times. "Call them, motherfucker," I told him. "They will take your ass to jail for harboring a fugitive when we find this bitch." But we couldn't find her. I was pissed off and stunned at the same time.

I started giving him a hard time, demanding to know where she was. I told him that I had heard her voice through the door, and he said that I must have heard the television. "The television isn't on, you lying piece of shit," one of the other agents pointed out. He tried to say that he turned it off when we knocked, but he was lying through his yellow teeth. That bitch was in here and I knew it. But where was she? We had torn the place apart. So, I really started studying the place. It wasn't very big. There was a small bedroom on the main floor, and a steep set of stairs leading up to another bedroom. There was a small closet under the stairs, but I had looked there both times. But when I really got to looking around, something didn't make sense. There was about two feet of space under those stairs that wasn't accounted for. I ripped all of the clothes out of that closet and really gave the walls a closer look. As I suspected, the closet ended about two feet short of the outside wall. There was a hidden room back there, and I knew that bitch was in it.

The closet walls were all made from that old school wooden paneling with the black grooves in it. But the black grooves didn't meet up properly with each other on the right side. I grabbed an umbrella out of the closet and started prying on the panels with the point. Dude immediately started to freak out and tried to charge me. The other two agents had to hold him off while I pried that paneling back enough for me to get a grip on it. But I wasn't going to have to do that at all. Our fugitive jumped out of there like a giant, crack head jack-in-the-box. We both came rolling out of that closet together and now the fight was three on two.

A few minutes earlier, when we were searching the place, I had pulled the couch bed out to look inside of it. Now, it was in everybody's way. There wasn't room for two people to be fighting in there, let alone five, so it all escalated very quickly. The other two guys were dealing with the boyfriend, and I was dealing with her. She was fighting me like a wild Indian. With no real room for me to move around, she somehow punched me in the face. I will give her some credit though, she knocked the shit out of me. I fell backwards onto the bed and she jumped right on top of me, throwing punches. I was done fighting this bitch. As soon as she landed on me, I rolled her over and pepper sprayed her. I gave her such a dose that it choked everyone in the room. The other two guys got the boyfriend out on the porch and one of them was actually sitting on him. The other one came in to help me cuff her, but that wasn't going to happen anytime soon. She was flailing around on the bed like she was possessed when dude tried to grab her. That's when this whole operation shifted gears. She bit the tip of his middle finger off.

So now, there's an agent sitting on an asshole on the porch, the both of them yelling at each other. She is still swinging her fists and screaming. I am choking half to death, and dude is yelling, "That bitch bit my finger off!" That's about when I saw my opportunity to stop this crazy train. It was a simple plan, really. I punched her right between the eyes. I hit her as hard as I could. She flipped off of the other side of the bed and hit the back of her head on an old school stereo system. She hit the floor and immediately had a seizure. Yep, I hadn't ended anything. I had just made shit worse. She was flopping around on the floor like a fish in a boat and ended up under the bed. Dude outside had his hands full with the boyfriend now, because he was screaming bloody murder. I think that's when the police got there.

I just want to say that I have no idea how to handle someone who's having a seizure. I will say that on this particular occasion, I decided that the best course of action was for me to just stand back and watch. The deputy that had arrived must have agreed, because he watched with me for a moment while I tried to explain what had happened. Finally, she quit whatever she was doing, and wrapped herself up in the steel bars under the bed. Three of us couldn't drag her out of there. Seriously, there was just no way to make her let go without hurting her, so the deputy came up with a bright idea. He called the fire department and an ambulance.

This whole thing had turned into a three-ring circus. The boyfriend had calmed down since the police arrived and we learned that a neighbor had called 911 about the disturbance. Another deputy had rolled in by then, and then here came the entire goddamn fire department. I remember joking with the other two agents because they had told me earlier that they wanted to keep their visit low key and under the radar. That ship had sailed.

I stayed out on the porch while the fire department and paramedics were inside doing their thing. They had carried all sorts of equipment inside and I'm not sure what the hell was going on. I know that one of the medics was inside trying to communicate with the fugitive, but she wasn't responding. The other was outside dealing with dude's finger, which wasn't nearly as bad as any of us thought. After a little while, two firemen carried old girl out onto the porch to us. I will never forget it as long as I live. She was still grasping that steel bar with her arms and legs and they had carried her out like a pig on a spit. Everyone laughed except her boyfriend. I don't know what his problem was, because that shit was hilarious. We simply slid her off the spit... I mean... pole, put the handcuffs on her, and shoved her into the ambulance. She had still never said a single word to anyone. The party broke up, two of us followed the ambulance, and old nine fingers rode inside with her.

We weren't in the emergency room very long at all. There was nothing seriously wrong with her. She had a knot on her forehead and a cut in her hair that needed a few stitches. Dude got a couple of stitches in his finger and they headed south with their fugitive and one hell of a story to tell their friends.

YOU TOTALED MY JEEP!

Like so many other stories, this one starts with a phone call from a tipster. The girl who called said that she had seen the fugitive's reward poster on Facebook and that she could easily lead me to him. She told me that he and a friend were actually coming to pick her up in a few hours and she offered to communicate with me by text from the vehicle. This was the exact definition of "inside information," so Bobby and I got ready to go. We didn't know where they were going, but we at least knew what area the caller lived in, so we headed to that general vicinity. The caller didn't want the fugitive to know that she was a rat, so she didn't want to give us her actual address. It didn't take long for her to text me as promised.

They had left her residence and were headed towards town on a main thoroughfare that we both knew very well. The tipster was texting me as she rode along, answering every question that I asked. The entire operation was actually going pretty well. She described the vehicle to me and said that there were three people inside. It was a two door SUV with a male driver, our tipster in the passenger seat, and our fugitive in the back seat. She said that they were going to stop at a particular nearby convenience store to pick up some beer. She said that she thought all three of them would probably go inside. We were close by, so we pulled into the parking lot and waited for them.

A few minutes later, the SUV pulled in and parked right in front of the entrance. I pulled up closer and waited for the doors to open. I wanted the driver to be clear of the vehicle before making a move. The second that the driver stepped out, I pulled in close to block them in and we jumped out. I went to the driver's side and Bobby went to the passenger's side. The fugitive was in the back seat, wearing a hoodie, with the hood pulled tight around his face. He was clearly trying to conceal his identity, but that wasn't going to work because I knew him well. We had both doors open and both front seats leaning forward when I drew my pistol on him. I yelled at him to put his hands where I could see them and ordered him to exit on the passenger's side. He did neither of these things immediately, and I was trying to tell him that there was nowhere for him to go. But he was going to do this the hard way.

He made a quick move, straightening his entire body out, and jammed both of his hands into his hoodie pockets. Now, here's where things get shady in this line of work. It's easy to sit at home, watch a body cam video, and say what you think the officer should have done. But, until it happens to you personally, your opinion means almost zero to those of us that deal with it regularly. I had no idea what was in those pockets, but I had to assume that it was a weapon. However, if I had shot him and it ended up just being a cell phone in his pocket, I would have been in deep shit. On the other hand, if I had waited long enough to actually see a gun, one of us could have been killed. Either way, I had a fraction of a second to decide which option to go with. I chose option three.

I dove into the vehicle, punched him in the side of the head, and grabbed his arms. All of that was no easy task. Remember, this was a two-door vehicle. There was barely enough room for your average crack whore to squeeze through there, but I somehow did it and the fight was on. I reached Bobby my gun, got that idiot into a headlock, and plowed out the passenger side with him still fighting me. Now, there was definitely not enough room for that. We went over the passenger seat together and we used every inch of that door opening to get out of that vehicle.

Now we were fighting on the ground in the parking lot. Dude was scrappy, but I never needed to hit him a second time. It was more of a wrestling match that ended with him handcuffed.

That's when I realized that someone was recording us. I didn't mind being recorded, but when it happens, that person rarely gets the entire story on video. Naturally, people don't record until after an incident has begun, and there's never any footage of how it all started. That was the case this time. Some mouthy bitch with a camera phone was yelling that she had us on tape beating that handcuffed man. What a crock of shit! The fight had been over the very second that we got cuffs on him. She just couldn't see that. But with her screaming over and over, "They beat that guy for no reason," someone else was now yelling that they had called the police.

We scooped the guy up and tossed him onto the hood my car to pat him down. I was actually anxious to see what was in those hoodie pockets that was important enough to damn near get him shot. He was running his mouth and cussing us out the entire time. The camera bitch was still yelling when I pulled two large bags of weed out of his pocket and tossed them onto my hood.

About that time, the driver of the SUV joined into the yelling match. He was saying, "Y'all totaled my fucking Jeep!" I couldn't figure out why he was saying that at first, but then I saw what he was talking about. I had never seen anything like it, actually. His passenger door was open. When I say it was open, I mean it was open all the way. The hinges had pulled out of the body, and the door itself was all the way forward, actually touching the front fender. He was right. That shitbox probably was totaled. But that wasn't my fault or my problem. Emotions were high, but I managed to get everyone to calm down long enough for the state police to arrive.

The trooper got everyone's side of the story and made short work of the entire bullshit call. He told the Jeep guy that if he hadn't been hauling around a wanted shithead, his Jeep wouldn't be fucked up. He also told him that he was free to sue me in civil court, but reminded him that this place had an excellent surveillance system and that he could never win that case anyway. He pretty much told the cell phone bitch to mind her damn business and that she had no idea what she was talking about. It also turned out that my fugitive actually had a separate set of warrants with the state police, so the trooper even took the guy into custody for me. Also, since the arrest was on video, the trooper was able to charge him with the drugs as well. It was literally a win, win, win situation for me, and I was about to learn that I had also dodged yet another bullet.

An hour or so later, the trooper called me on my cell phone. He was in the emergency room with the defendant, who had several shattered bones in one of his hands. The defendant was raising hell and now threatening to sue everyone involved. The broken hand was news to me and I couldn't figure out how it might have happened. Later, I mentioned the broken hand to the tipster when I called her to arrange the reward payment. She said, "Oh yeah, he broke it a few days ago, working on a tractor." So, none of us had broken it after all, but I'm sure the fight had aggravated it and made it worse. Before it was all over with, the trooper got with her for a written statement. It turned out that she actually had text messages with the fugitive about the previously broken hand, so we were all in the clear.

FISH FUCKERS REVISITED

I want to end this second book by addressing a few of the emails that I have received about the first one. Specifically, emails about the Fish Fucker chapter. For those of you who may not have read my first book, I told a story about a "gentleman" who I saw fucking a fish. I never actually met the guy and do not know him at all, so I'm throwing the word "gentleman" out there for lack of a better word. I would like to think that aside from someone who fucks fish, maybe he could be otherwise pretty well rounded. Dude could be a deacon in his church for all I know. I mean, Genesis 1:28 says that God's own words were, "Be fruitful, multiply, and have dominion over the fish of the sea." Although somehow, in my heart, I just don't think this is what he meant.

I have received emails from two angry readers who have threatened to sue me over that chapter. Let me explain why that's not possible. I did not mention any names in that story, nor did I even suggest the area where the incident happened. That alone holds me harmless from any threats of legal action. But more importantly, the story wasn't even about either of the two "gentlemen" that sent those angry emails. This all raises a few troubling questions.

First, just how many of you people are out there fucking fish? I mean, getting two emails from folks that I have never met tells me that fish fucking must be a much more popular hobby than I would have ever guessed. Maybe that's why the aquariums at those big sporting goods stores are so popular. That must be like big-screen, high-definition porn to you weirdos.

Second, if you do fuck fish, and you think that I might have saw you, why would you email me and complain that I wrote about it? I didn't mention any names, so why not just remain silent about it? Emailing me just brings attention to yourself and now I know your secret. It makes no sense to me, but neither does fish fucking, so I'm not going to second guess your logic.

Third, how are fish fuckers even reading my books? I can't imagine that any of them have a decent job and I intentionally tried to set the price out of their range. That is, unless they are out there in all walks of life, like in that Fight Club movie. I would like to think that my doctor and my mailman aren't out there fucking fish on their days off. Are there meetings? Is rule number one about fish fucking to never talk about fish fucking? If so, I imagine that emailing me about it would be a clear violation.

Made in the USA
Middletown, DE
18 September 2024

61143610R00119